THE MYSTIC MOUNTAIN

A POETIC SCENARIO

BY
DUNSTAN MASSEY

FOR THE RESURRECTION

First edition 2002
08 07 06 05 04 03 02 7 6 5 4 3 2 1

ISBN 1-903689-02-3

Published by Piquant
PO Box 83, Carlisle, CA3 9GR, United Kingdom
www.piquant.net info@piquant.net

A catalogue record of this book is available in the UK
from the British Library, in the USA from the Library
of Congress and in Canada from the National Library
of Canada.

Reproduction: Gazelle Creative Productions Ltd
Cover image: Dunstan Massey, *Mount Tabor* from
'Inner Dialogue', tempera
Cover design: Jonathan Kearney

CONTENTS

ACKNOWLEDGEMENTS

It is as much a pleasure as a duty to thank all those many who have helped:

Rt. Rev. Maurus Macrae, Abbot of Westminster at Mission in British Columbia, Canada, for his kind approval of this work for publication;

Confreres Fr Basil Foote and Fr Alban Riley, for proofreading and secretarial work, and Br Peter Jamin for his photography;

Miss Rhonda Wood, for her dedicated word processing of many drafts;

Canadian composer Elliot Weisgarber, for his permission to reprint his choral setting of the Latin stanzas from the first five sequences;

Michael Young, American organist and composer, for permission to publish his setting of the Jewel stanzas from Sequence Seven;

Dr Loren Wilkinson of Regent College, Vancouver, for initiating and supporting this project;

Dr Gerald Morgan, Seminary of Christ the King faculty, for writing the preface to the book;

Elria and Pieter Kwant of the publishing house of Piquant in England, for their most helpful and enthusiastic collaboration.

PREFACE

The great heads of Presidents hewn on Mount Rushmore strike awe in the viewer; but, set in the Grand Canyon (where Time is rock and the fish in it), those totems would be pygmies. Compared with Dakota sacredness on which they intrude, the colossi are petty things and fleeting. What if the whole sacred Mountain were man-shaped: were Christ, too vast to be seen by touring in flesh alive? Father Dunstan Massey widens the scope further, for a Mountain absorbing all others rooted under sea (like Sinai, Popocatepetl, Anapurna, Carmel, Cassino) to harbour all as Mystic Mountain of Psalm 17: God is my rock. As with Dante's mountain of Purgatory, the form is barely known to earthlings made alien alive.

The vastness unveiled by anyone's death is offered in the form of a dynamic vision of complex magnitude. Fr Dunstan's art is long practiced in harmonic drama. His oil-painting *Mountain Storm* dates from the year after his one-man show at the Vancouver Art Gallery at the age of 16, the year before his first poems were written in 1942. He was soon at large-scale symbolic painting, and ink-drawn illustrations of Dante — whose work he staged while teaching Drama, Philosophy and Liturgy. After an *Ordination* in tempera came his own Ordination in 1955, when he had just completed sixteen poured-concrete reliefs for the ceiling of the monastery common room.

The Resurrection-theme of *The Mystic Mountain* has been a constant for Fr Dunstan, who scripted the live CBC telecast of the Abbey's paschal liturgy in 1957; he designed the faceted stained-glass *Resurrection* window for the bell tower crypt in 1958, combining this with his Latin and English poetry for a proposed but unproduced film. *The Mystic Mountain* grew from this film script, Phoenix-like, in the years when he was occupied drawing 250 animations for yet another film. In this period he completed a large fresco for the cloister (1974), besides 22 cast-cement reliefs for the new abbey church from 1980 to 1994. His film *Crown of Fire* won the Golden Eagle at the Cine Awards in Washington D.C. in 1998, and meanwhile the book was made ready for press.

The soul's analogue in bone and stone, borne through grave and ocean's deep to Revelation's height, is art from long contemplation.

Dr Gerald Morgan
Seminary Faculty Member
West Vancouver, 2002

But some man will say, 'How are the dead raised? With what manner of body do they come?' Senseless man, that which thou sowest is not quickened, except it die: and that which thou sowest, thou sowest not the body that shall be, but bare grain, perhaps of wheat, or of some other grain. But God giveth it a body as he will, and to every seed its own body. All flesh is not the same flesh, but there is one kind of flesh of men, another of beasts, another of birds, another of fishes. There are celestial bodies, and bodies terrestrial; but the glory of the celestial is one, and the glory of the terrestrial is another. There is one glory of the sun, and another glory of the moon, and another glory of the stars. For star differeth from star in glory. So also is the resurrection of the dead. What is sown in corruption, is raised in incorruption. It is sown in dishonour, it is raised in glory. It is sown in weakness, it is raised in power. It is sown a natural body, it is raised a spiritual body. If there be a natural body, there is also a spiritual body. Thus it is written, 'The first man Adam was made into a living soul', the last Adam into a quickening spirit. Yet that was not first which is spiritual, but that which is natural, and afterward that which is spiritual. The first man was of the earth, earthy; the second man is from heaven. As was the earthy, such are they also that are earthy; and as is the heavenly, such are they also that are heavenly. Just as we have borne the image of the earthy, we shall also bear the image of the heavenly.

Now this I say, brethren, that flesh and blood cannot inherit the kingdom of God; neither shall corruption inherit incorruption. Behold, I tell you a mystery. We shall not all sleep, but we shall all be changed, in a moment, in the twinkling of an eye, at the last trumpet. For the trumpet shall sound, and the dead shall be raised incorruptible, and we shall be changed. For this corruptible must put on incorruption, and this mortal must put on immortality. And when this corruptible puts on incorruption, and this mortal puts on immortality, then shall come to pass the saying that is written.

'Death is swallowed up in victory.'
'O death, where is thy victory?
O death, where is thy sting?'

1 Corinthians 15:35-55

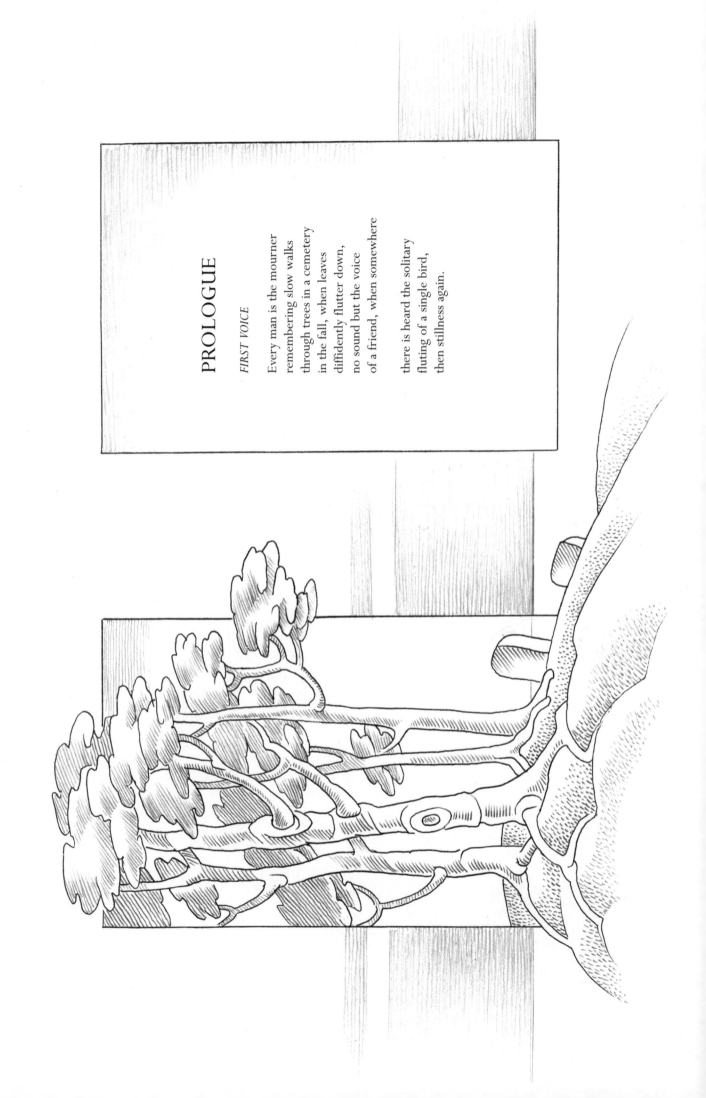

PROLOGUE

FIRST VOICE

Every man is the mourner
remembering slow walks
through trees in a cemetery
in the fall, when leaves
diffidently flutter down,
no sound but the voice
of a friend, when somewhere

there is heard the solitary
fluting of a single bird,
then stillness again.

SECOND VOICE

When you were a child
you buried your dead
robins with ceremony.

'I'll cushion his wings
with moss,'
         you said,
'I'll cover him
with leaves and loam
for he is just asleep.

Sing, bird —
         sing, little bird.'

You remember the song,
my friend?
         the innocent hope?

THE MOURNER

You speak of hope. Shattering
blows have buried my hope,
my birdsong. My faith, I fear,
is perilously near extinction.

THIRD VOICE

And walking, we find ourselves
in the empty house, with its
cruciform window casting
shadow on the floor.

THE MOURNER

Have I any reason for canticles?
When wise theologians
claiming to be good
Christians, as they do, yet

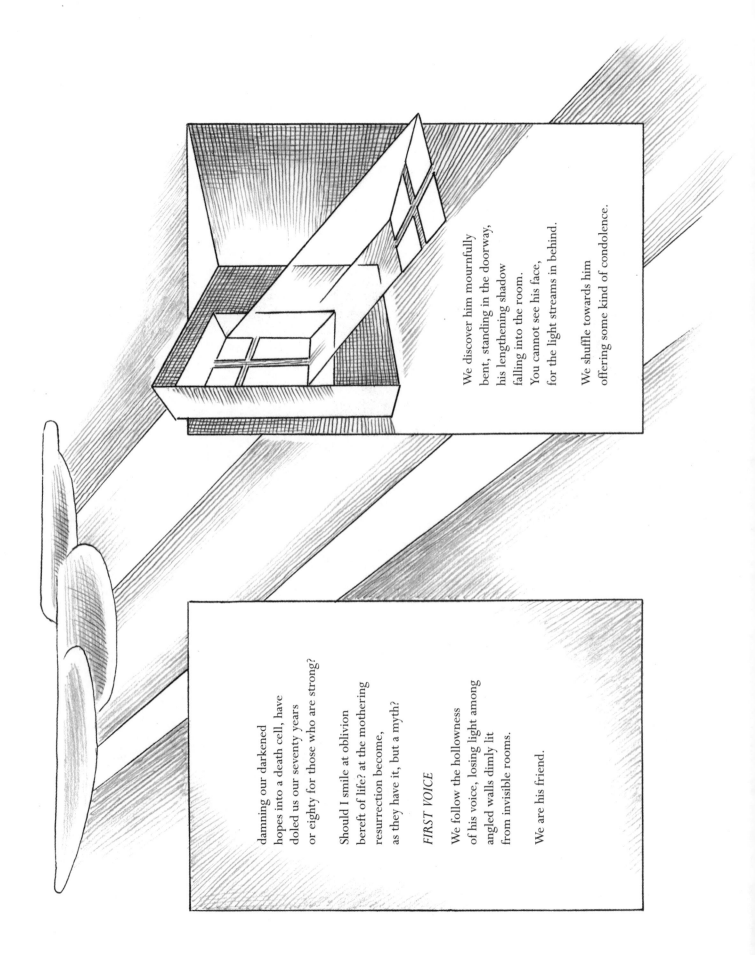

damming our darkened
hopes into a death cell, have
doled us our seventy years
or eighty for those who are strong?

Should I smile at oblivion
bereft of life? at the mothering
resurrection become,
as they have it, but a myth?

FIRST VOICE

We follow the hollowness
of his voice, losing light among
angled walls dimly lit
from invisible rooms.

We are his friend.

We discover him mournfully
bent, standing in the doorway,
his lengthening shadow
falling into the room.
You cannot see his face,
for the light streams in behind.

We shuffle towards him
offering some kind of condolence.

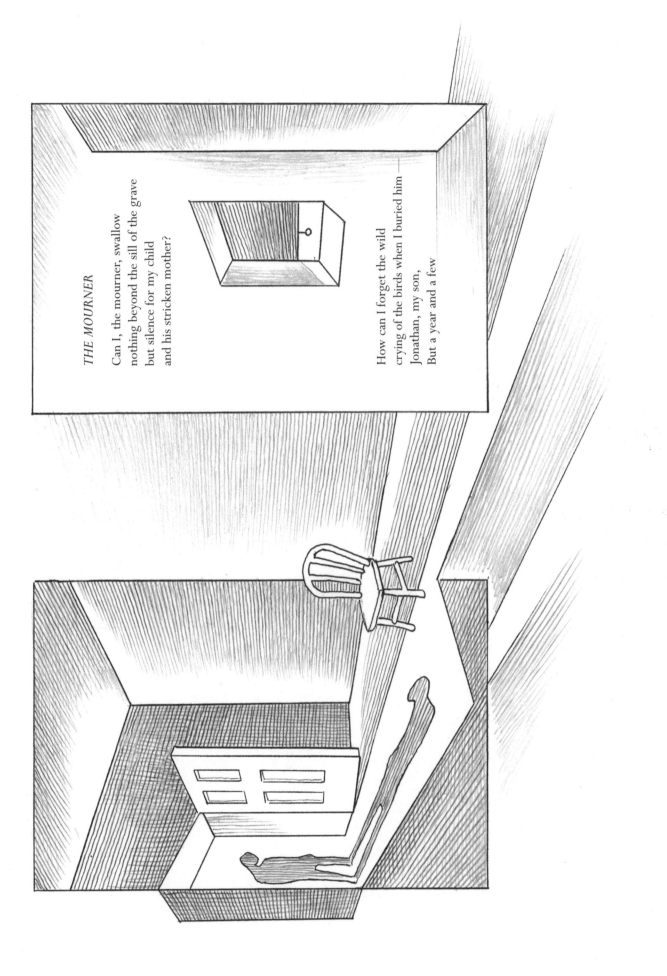

THE MOURNER

Can I, the mourner, swallow
nothing beyond the sill of the grave
but silence for my child
and his stricken mother?

How can I forget the wild
crying of the birds when I buried him —
Jonathan, my son,
But a year and a few

THE MOURNER

I'd forgotten the sparrows.
I can only remember
return to this empty house
where I walk, in my

desolate dreams,
those empty streets
in search of a door
my son left ajar.

FIRST VOICE

Numbed, we stalk
the deserted street with its
blind windows and doors locked,
are shocked in the gates
we pass through
as bearers enter, a coffin
between them,

terrifying weeks
without warning, after
laying under the loam
my Miriam under the leaves?

THIRD VOICE

As tears blur his figure
into a face, listening and lost,
we turn from the room
with a cane chair only
and a blind drawn against noon.

SECOND VOICE

You remember, my friend,
the five sparrows
sold for two farthings?

and not one of them
forgotten before God?

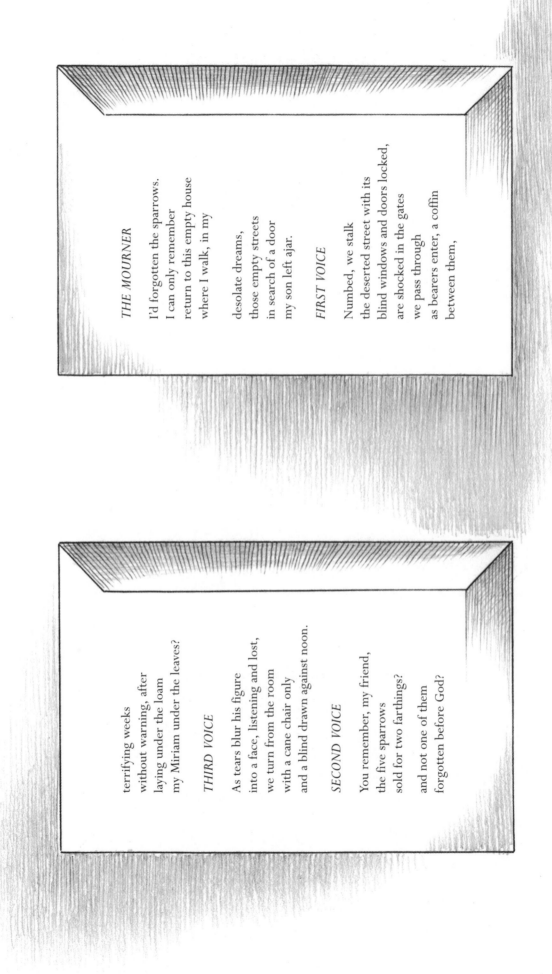

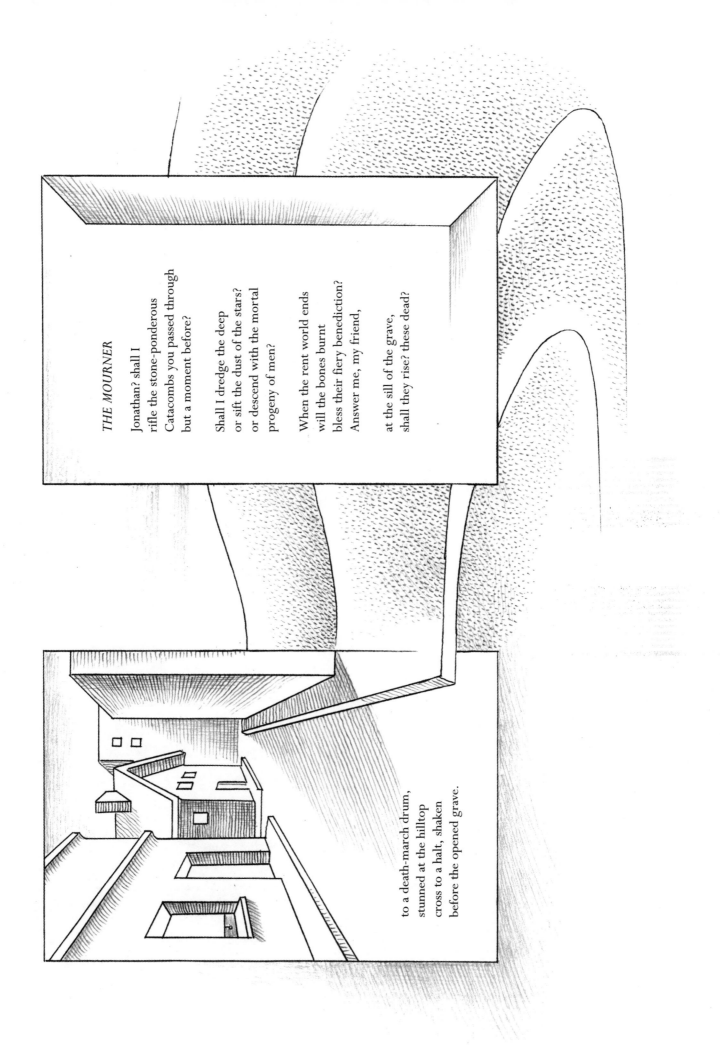

THE MOURNER

Jonathan? shall I
rifle the stone-ponderous
Catacombs you passed through
but a moment before?

Shall I dredge the deep
or sift the dust of the stars?
or descend with the mortal
progeny of men?

When the rent world ends
will the bones burnt
bless their fiery benediction?
Answer me, my friend,

at the sill of the grave,
shall they rise? these dead?

to a death-march drum,
stunned at the hilltop
cross to a halt, shaken
before the opened grave.

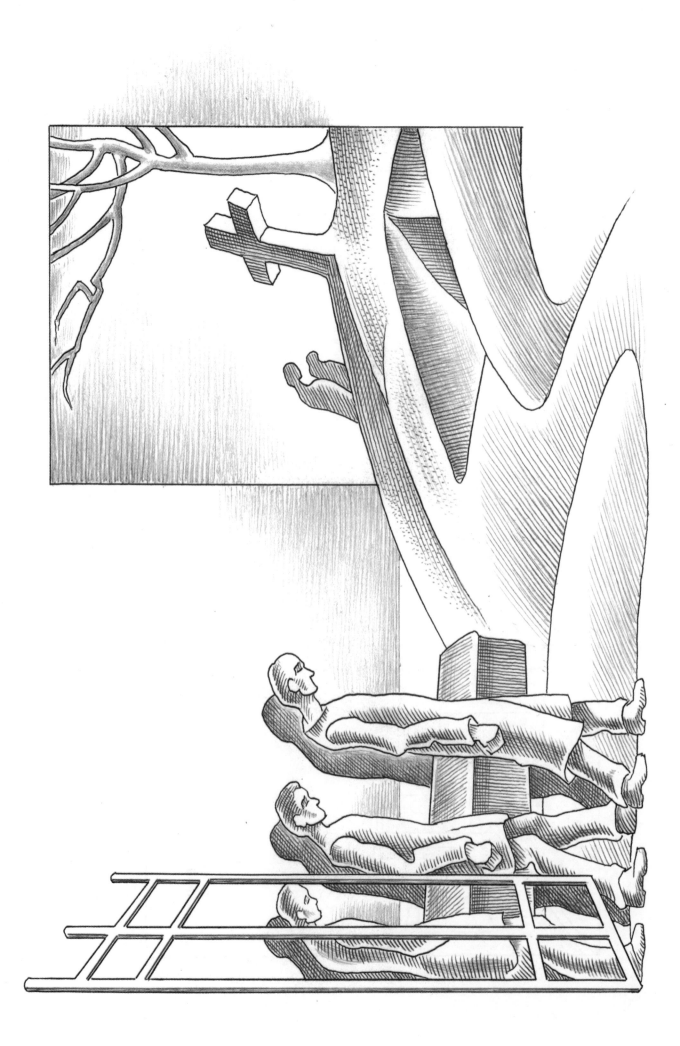

SEQUENCE ONE

A descent into the underworld where the Mourner sees his son passing through death's doorway into a field where a sower is casting seed which grows into a garden, into a child in the womb, into a mouldering tomb full of bones. Shocked, he sees himself staring down into his son's grave.

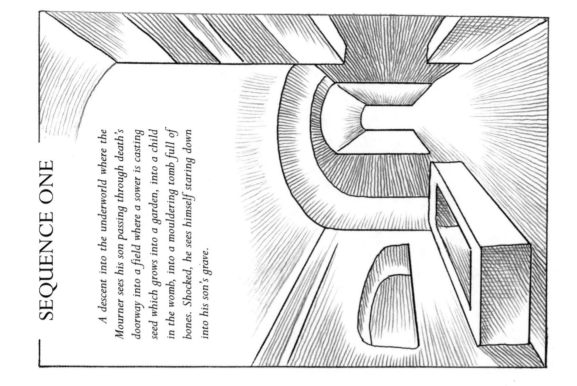

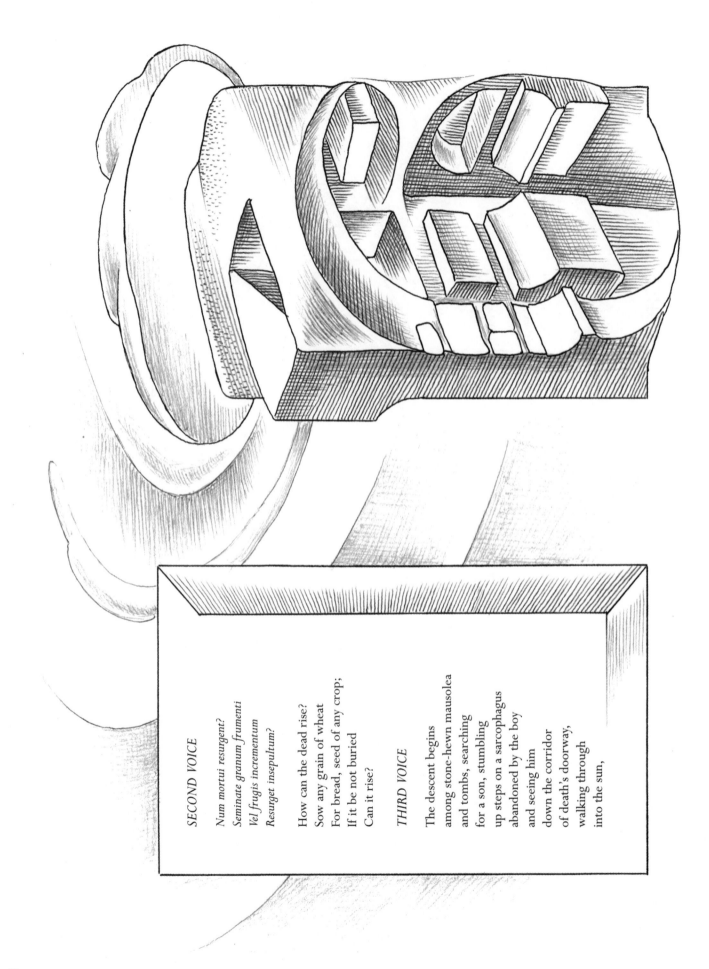

SECOND VOICE

Num mortui resurgent?
Seminate granum frumenti
Vel frugis incrementum
Resurget insepultum?

How can the dead rise?
Sow any grain of wheat
For bread, seed of any crop;
If it be not buried
Can it rise?

THIRD VOICE

The descent begins
among stone-hewn mausolea
and tombs, searching
for a son, stumbling
up steps on a sarcophagus
abandoned by the boy
and seeing him
down the corridor
of death's doorway,
walking through
into the sun,

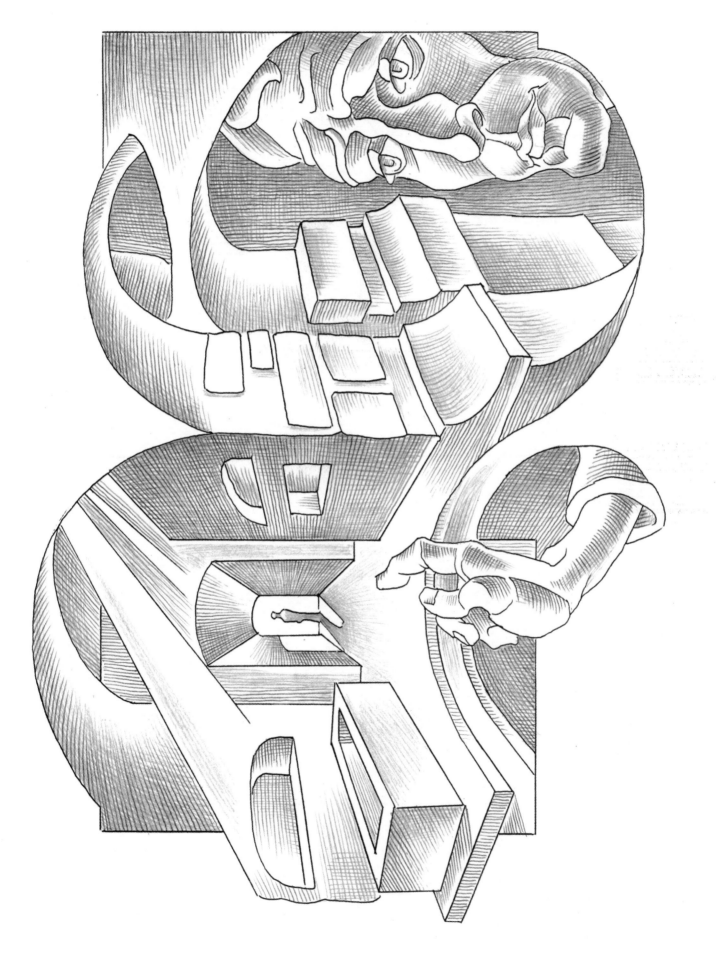

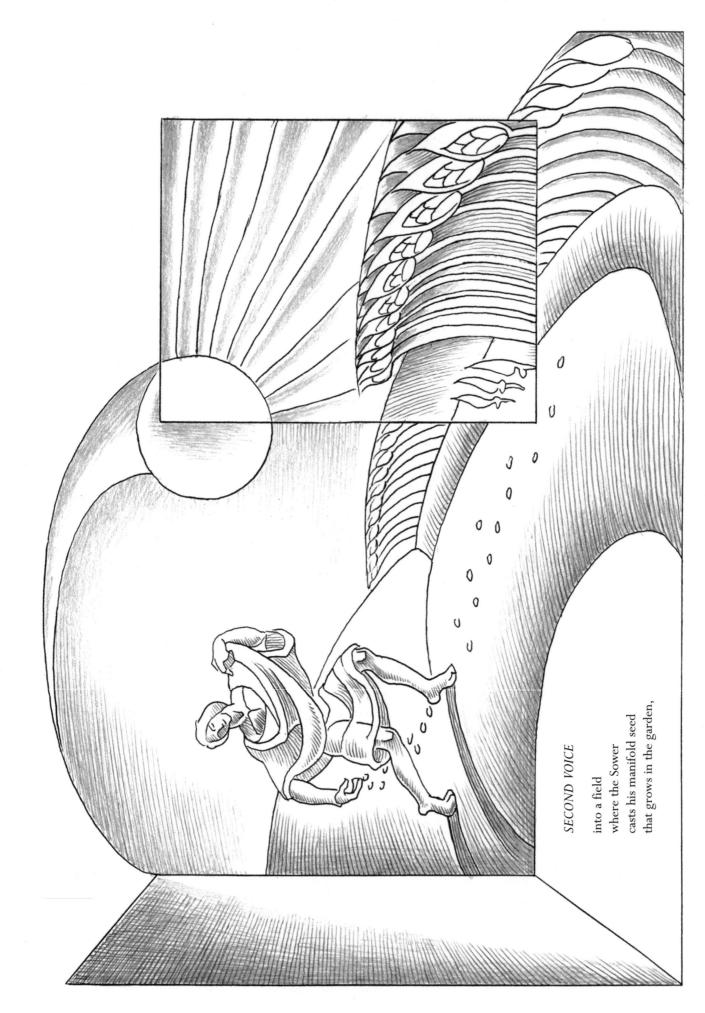

SECOND VOICE

into a field
where the Sower
casts his manifold seed
that grows in the garden,

22

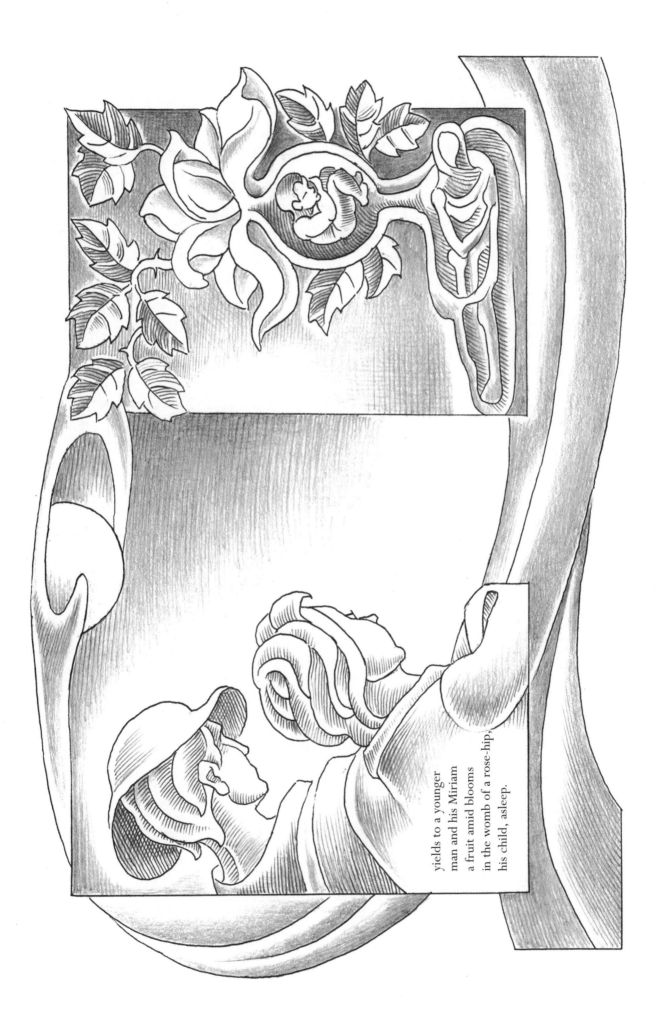

yields to a younger
man and his Miriam
a fruit amid blooms
in the womb of a rose-hip,
his child, asleep.

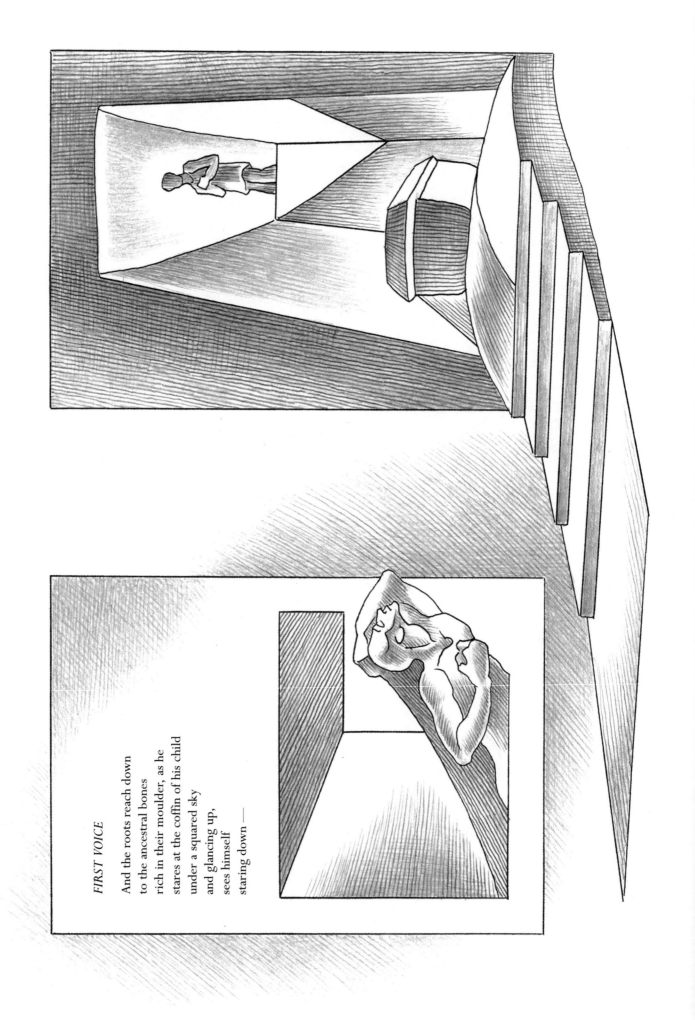

FIRST VOICE

And the roots reach down
to the ancestral bones
rich in their moulder, as he
stares at the coffin of his child
under a squared sky
and glancing up,
sees himself
staring down —

24

SEQUENCE TWO

A long dream, opening with gulls soaring over the sea. The Mourner moves into the city, now strangely empty of men warned, perhaps, of imminent disaster. The street falls away revealing the whole population descending stairs toward the door of death. His son passes through into the sea, so he follows. It is a place of metamorphosis, an allegory for baptism into death and resurrection. He finally discovers his child, asleep, in death's garden, at the bottom of the sea.

SECOND VOICE

*Cuique corpus proprium
Omni terrenoque;
Homini incolenti,
Natanti in profundo.*

Each its own body has,
Each earthly
Seed; Man on
The earth, and down
The fishes, deep.

FIRST VOICE

On the brink of death
it is well to divert
the distraught mind awhile,
to alert the eye to the turning
of leaves, to the winged whirling
of maple seeds or the soft
dropping of acorns.

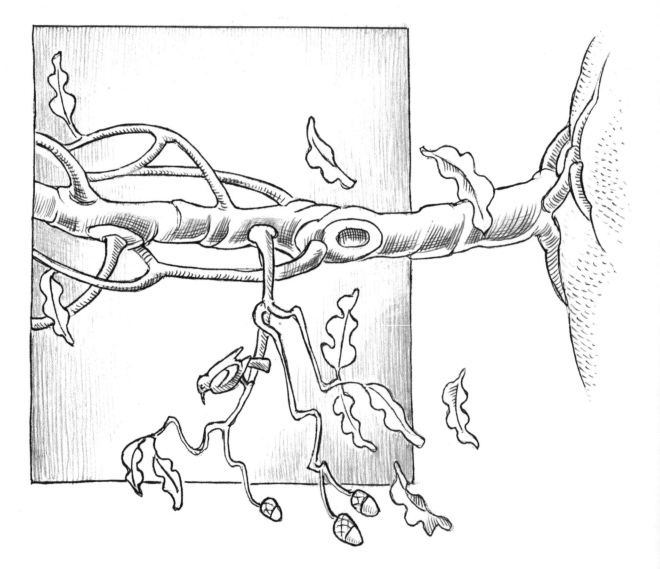

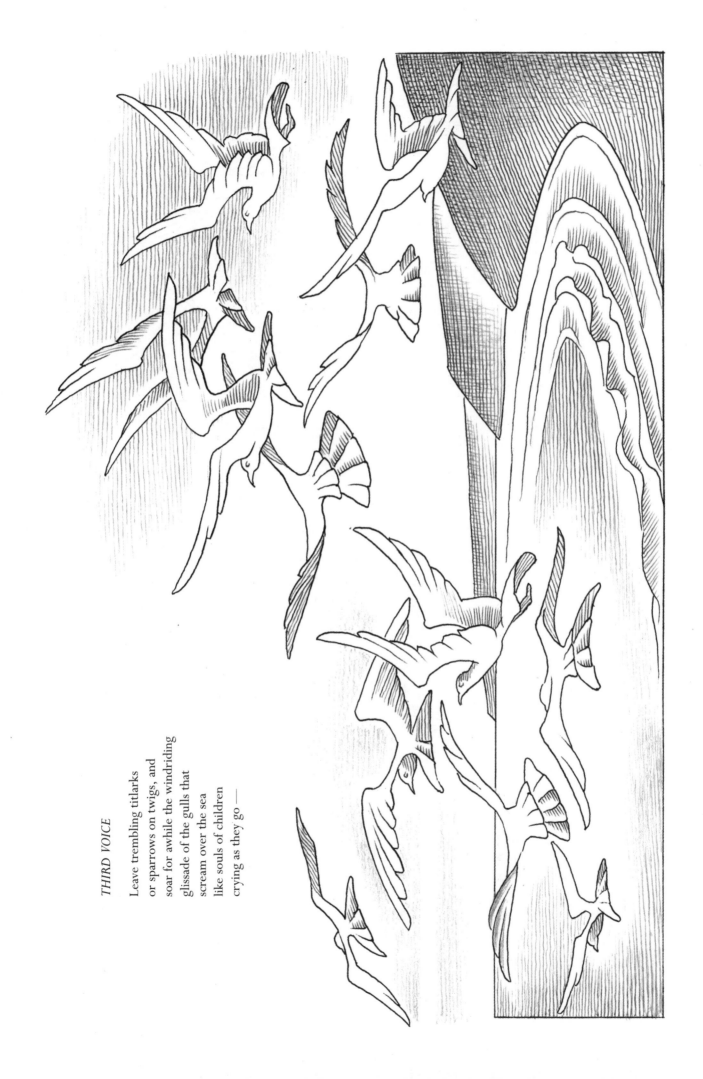

THIRD VOICE

Leave trembling titlarks
or sparrows on twigs, and
soar for awhile the windriding
glissade of the gulls that
scream over the sea
like souls of children
crying as they go —

27

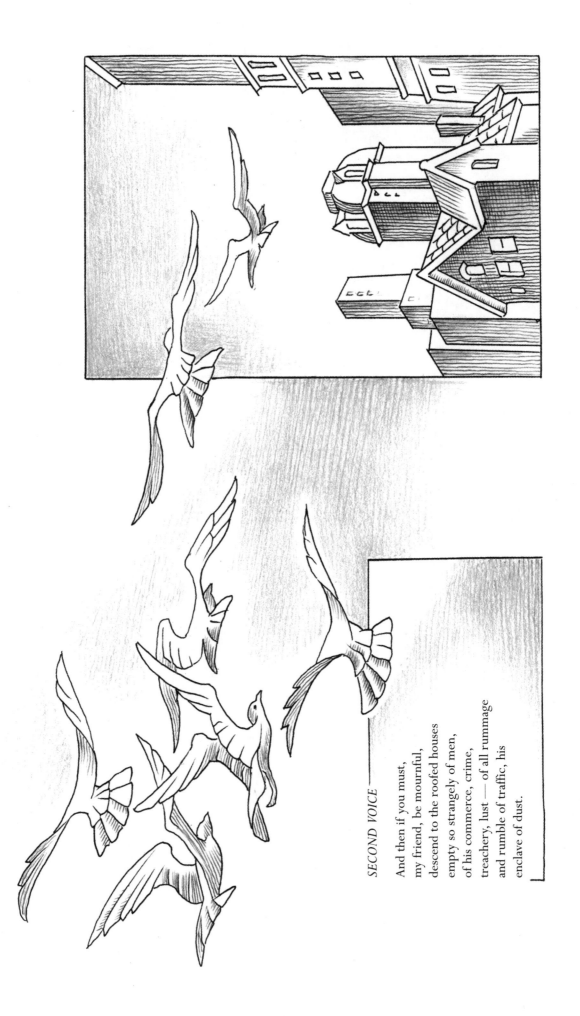

SECOND VOICE

And then if you must,
my friend, be mournful,
descend to the roofed houses
empty so strangely of men,
of his commerce, crime,
treachery, lust — of all rummage
and rumble of traffic, his
enclave of dust.

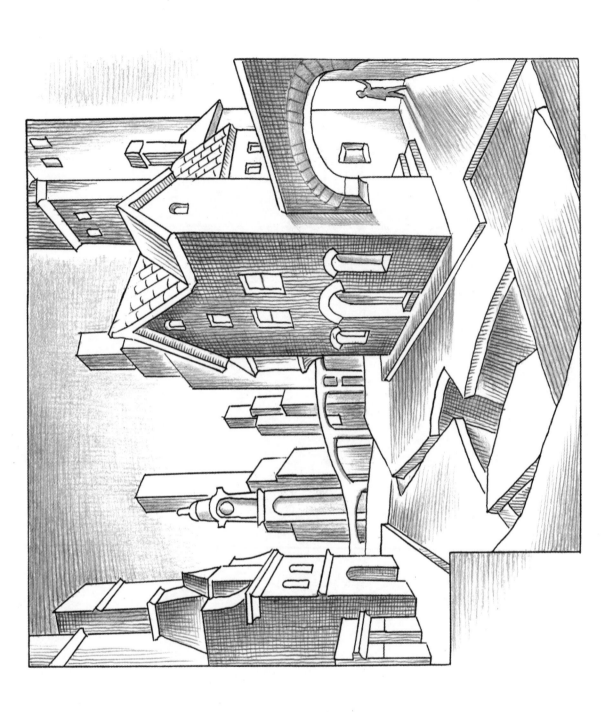

THIRD VOICE

Does the pavement buckle?
Does it sway underfoot,
shuddering as unstable
sands give way to a subterranean
collapse of culverts,
water mains, subway tunnels
or mines, all lathered
in a wash of the weltering sea?

Does he glide like a surfer
steadying his fragment of asphalt
falling, with feet that have learned
through a lifetime of nightmares
this manner of flight?

FIRST VOICE

He sounds the cavernous
escape of the race, down
the vertebrate ladder of bones
in a pelvic hollowness, this
staircase of stone, inching
the doomed and foetal generation
toward a watery orifice of death.

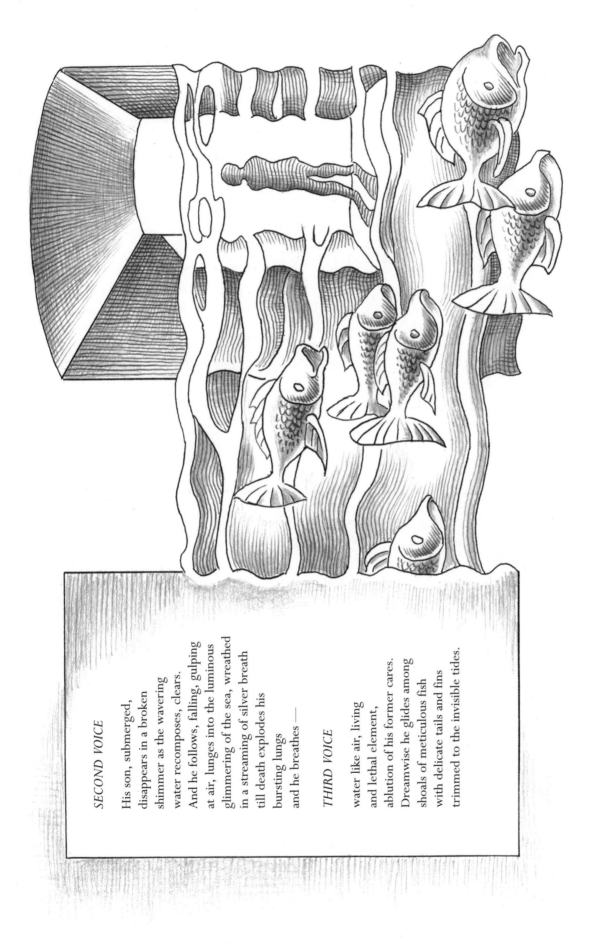

SECOND VOICE

His son, submerged,
disappears in a broken
shimmer as the wavering
water recomposes, clears.
And he follows, falling, gulping
at air, lunges into the luminous
glimmering of the sea, wreathed
in a streaming of silver breath
till death explodes his
bursting lungs
and he breathes —

THIRD VOICE

water like air, living
and lethal element,
ablution of his former cares.
Dreamwise he glides among
shoals of meticulous fish
with delicate tails and fins
trimmed to the invisible tides.

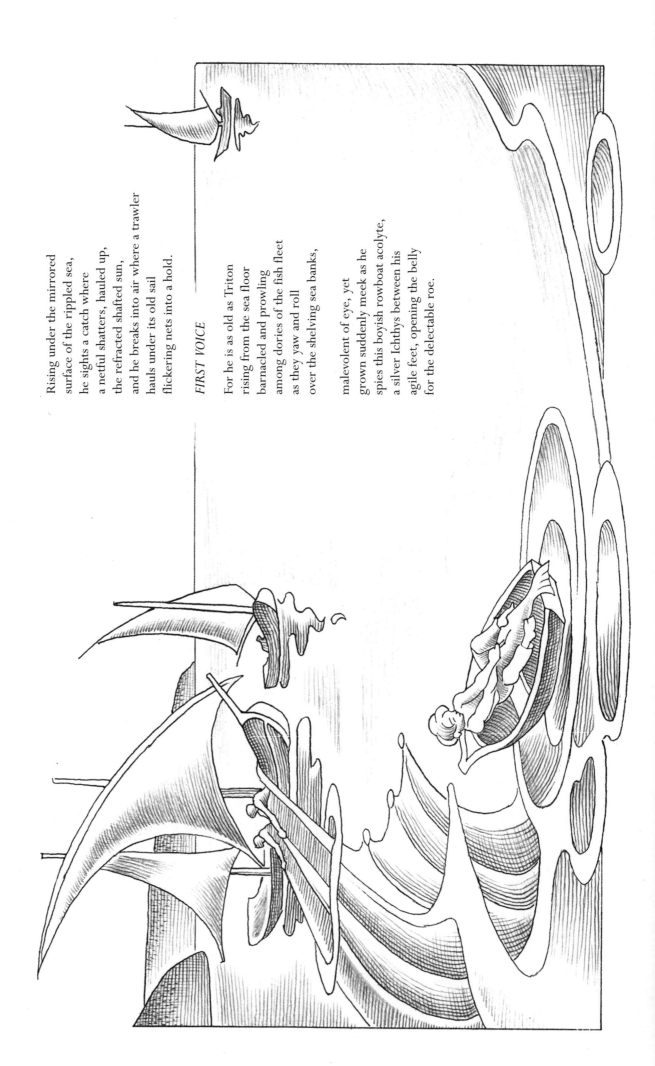

Rising under the mirrored
surface of the rippled sea,
he sights a catch where
a netful shatters, hauled up,
the refracted shafted sun,
and he breaks into air where a trawler
hauls under its old sail
flickering nets into a hold.

FIRST VOICE

For he is as old as Triton
rising from the sea floor
barnacled and prowling
among dories of the fish fleet
as they yaw and roll
over the shelving sea banks,

malevolent of eye, yet
grown suddenly meek as he
spies this boyish rowboat acolyte,
a silver Ichthys between his
agile feet, opening the belly
for the delectable roe.

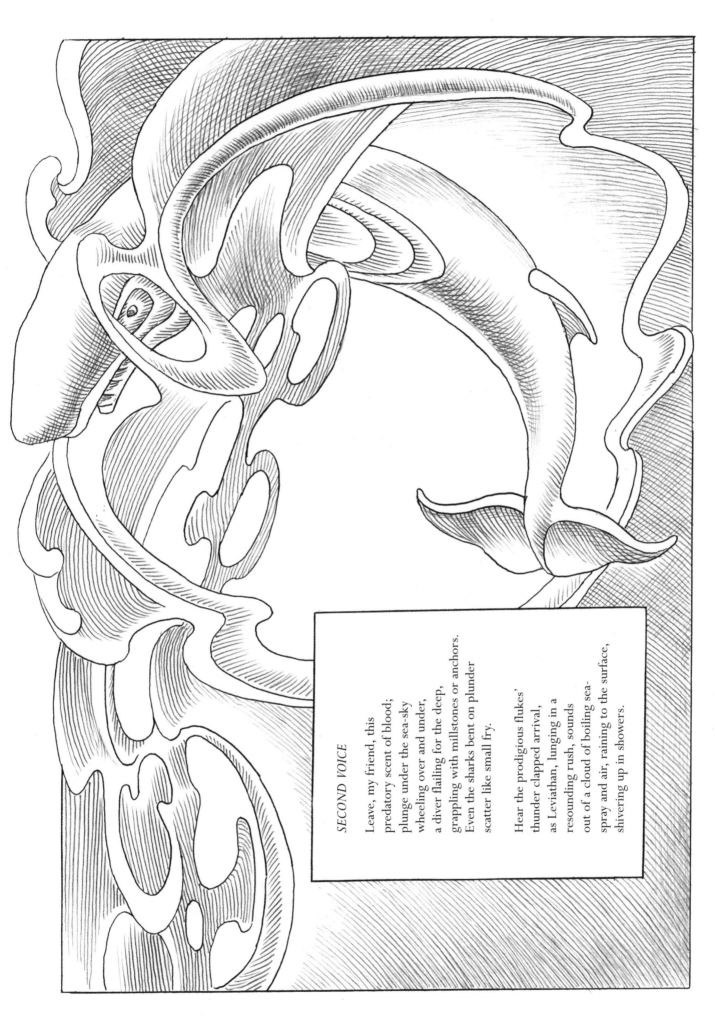

SECOND VOICE

Leave, my friend, this
predatory scent of blood;
plunge under the sea-sky
wheeling over and under,
a diver flailing for the deep,
grappling with millstones or anchors.
Even the sharks bent on plunder
scatter like small fry.

Hear the prodigious flukes'
thunder clapped arrival,
as Leviathan, lunging in a
resounding rush, sounds
out of a cloud of boiling sea-
spray and air, raining to the surface,
shivering up in showers.

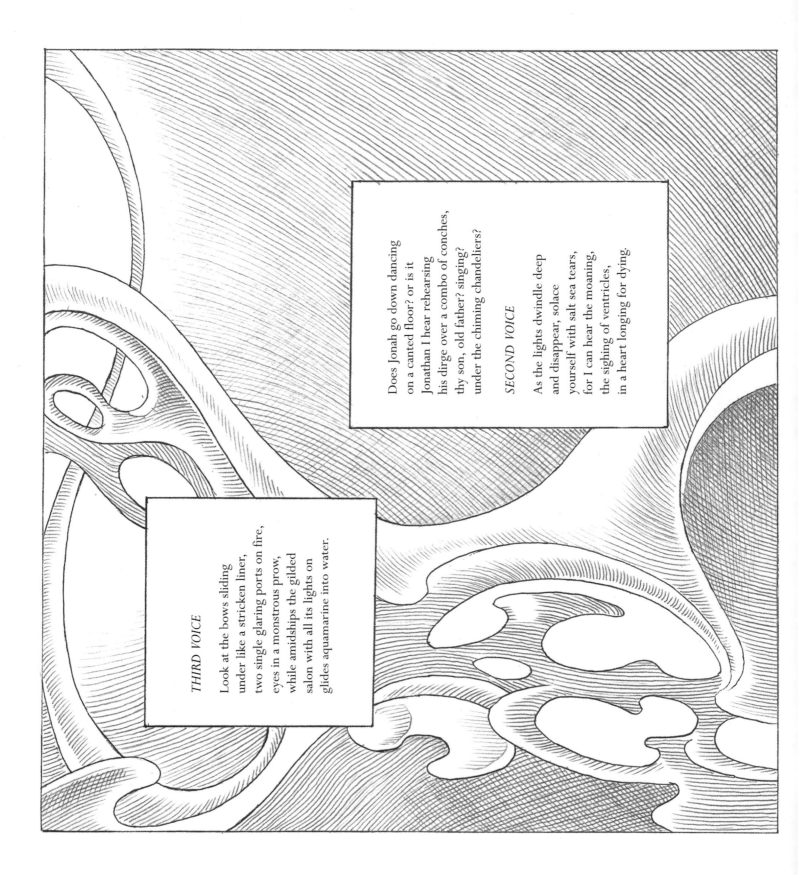

Does Jonah go down dancing
on a canted floor? or is it
Jonathan I hear rehearsing
his dirge over a combo of conches,
thy son, old father? singing?
under the chiming chandeliers?

SECOND VOICE

As the lights dwindle deep
and disappear, solace
yourself with salt sea tears,
for I can hear the moaning,
the sighing of ventricles,
in a heart longing for dying.

THIRD VOICE

Look at the bows sliding
under like a stricken liner,
two single glaring ports on fire,
eyes in a monstrous prow,
while amidships the gilded
salon with all its lights on
glides aquamarine into water.

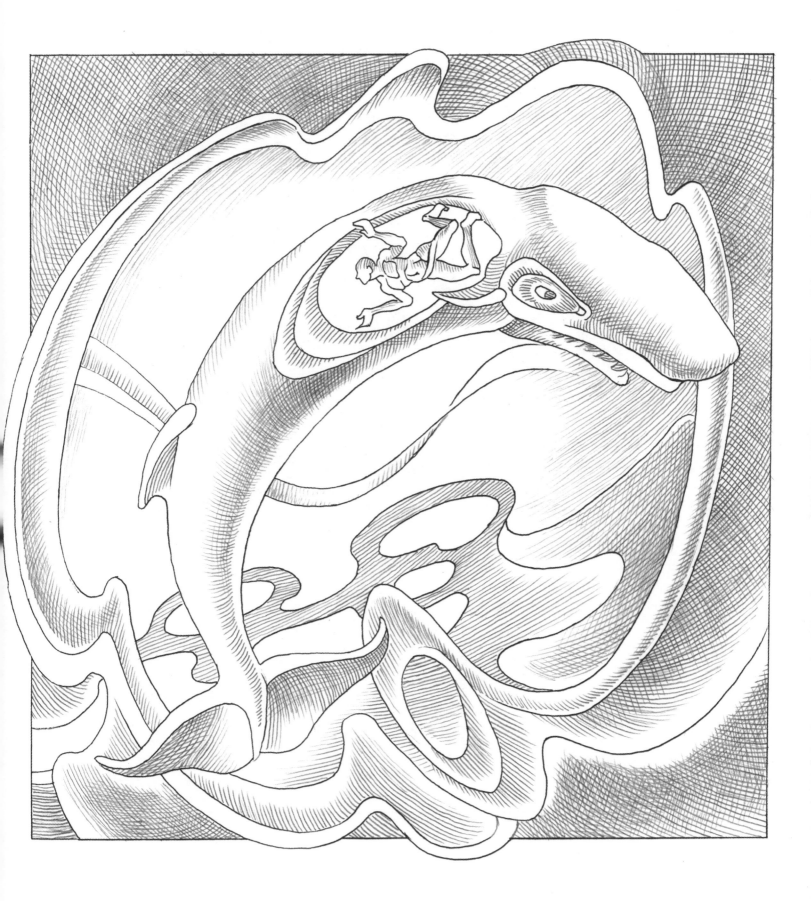

FIRST VOICE

Magnify with a glass-
blown lens for the eye
the miniature mayhem
of these paleozoic survivals
of the primal sea,

all monstrous phosphorescent
animalcula, diatom and hydra,
epicene generations devouring
and being devoured, forage
for the shrimp and krill,

that scatter to the raiding
viper of the deep, luminescent
Saracen, agile in depredation,
scimitared and snapping
his crystal teeth.

THIRD VOICE

Leave the anchor to the light,
its hawser to be heaved
deep out of the dusk, and come,
my friend, into the garden of night,

where volcanoes spilled their
fiery cylinders, entrails of molten magma
with explosive fracture, molting
sea stone ages ago, where

polyps grow an engulfed
cathedral known to seamen only,
who can hear under the slow
swell, a tolling of stone bells.

SECOND VOICE

In this claustral stillness
tread lightly, lest you wake
some skull impaled in a pearl,
or coral diadem of death.

Tread quietly the slumbrous
garden, lest you rouse
this man-child of the deep, asleep
in his silvered veil of sand,

with his triton, unwinded,
slipped from a nerveless hand,
his limbs forever slender,
twined in dreamless time,

his head forever drowsing, cushioned
in a shell, lest you trouble
his simple sleep, toll ever
so gently, sombre bell.

SEQUENCE THREE

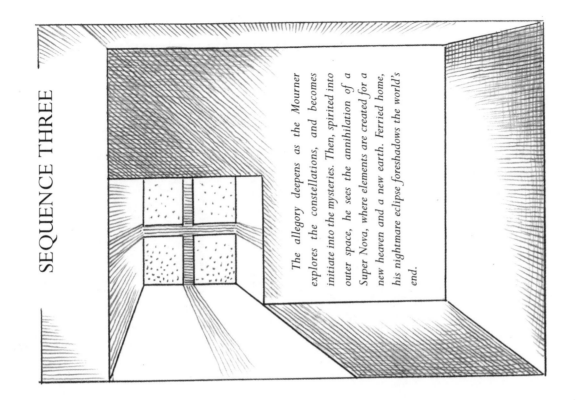

The allegory deepens as the Mourner explores the constellations, and becomes initiate into the mysteries. Then, spirited into outer space, he sees the annihilation of a Super Nova, where elements are created for a new heaven and a new earth. Ferried home, his nightmare eclipse foreshadows the world's end.

FIRST VOICE

Waking by the window
he is startled and alone,
for we are hidden, unseen,
on this clear midnight
when moonlight frosts
the stillness of the room.

THE MOURNER

My dearest, wherever you are,
whatever stars there are that
dance over the whirlwind leaves,

in the woods where you walked,
remember? do you see them now?
so busy with the rustle of chickadees?

Can you hear my crying
Miriam? this fall full of sighing
for Jonathan? a shell now in the sea —

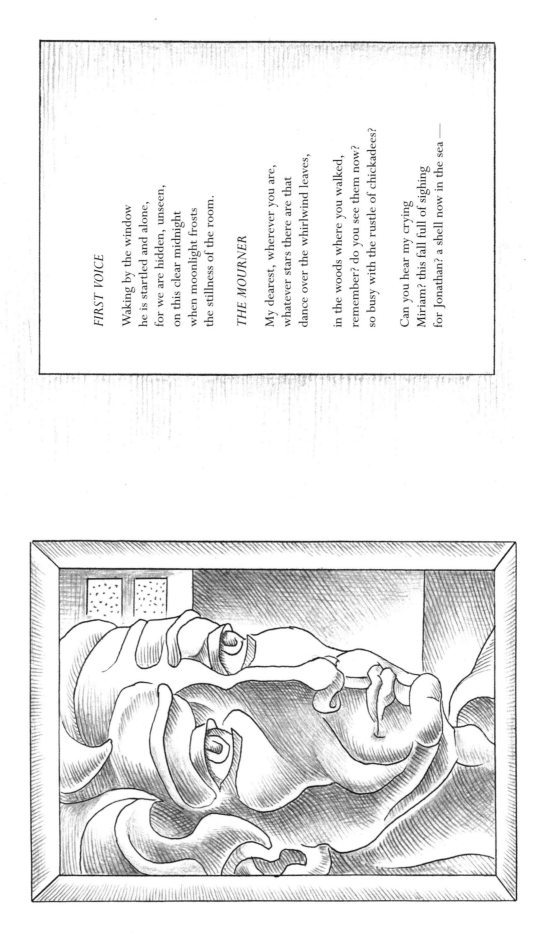

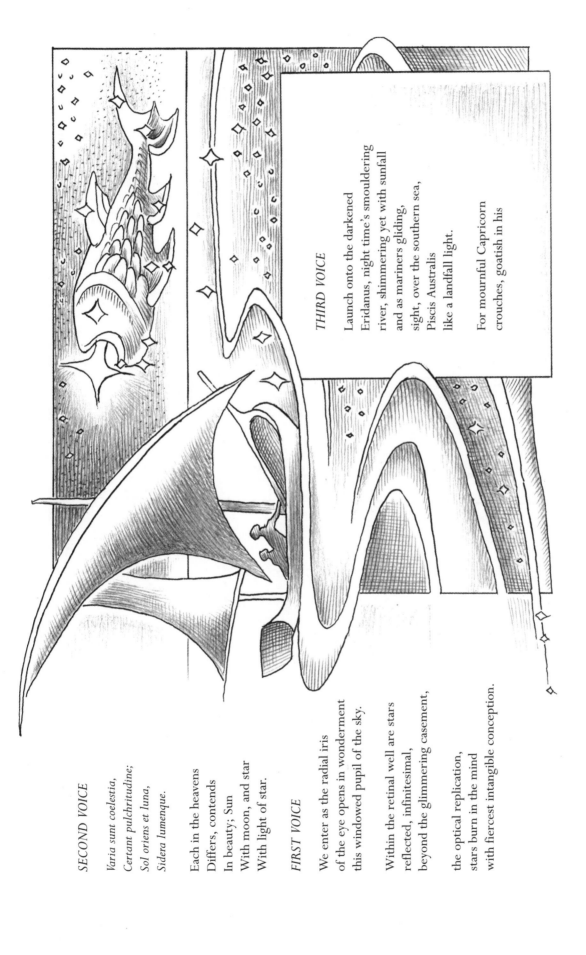

SECOND VOICE

Varia sunt coelestia,
Certant pulchritudine;
Sol oriens et luna,
Sidera lumenque.

Each in the heavens
Differs, contends
In beauty; Sun
With moon, and star
With light of star.

FIRST VOICE

We enter as the radial iris
of the eye opens in wonderment
this windowed pupil of the sky.

Within the retinal well are stars
reflected, infinitesimal,
beyond the glimmering casement,

the optical replication,
stars burn in the mind
with fiercest intangible conception.

THIRD VOICE

Launch onto the darkened
Eridanus, night time's smouldering
river, shimmering yet with sunfall
and as mariners gliding,
sight, over the southern sea,
Piscis Australis
like a landfall light.

For mournful Capricorn
crouches, goatish in his

41

panic disguise, as the wind-
whipped girl in sea chains,
Andromeda, awaits her
deliverer — of another name.

FIRST VOICE

While wintry Aquarius, his
hair full of rain, storm-charged
but of sanguine heart, resounds
with a voice glacial and dark
as starfalls tumble like
struck bells, the water jar rings.

There is one who stands among you;
make way for the ecliptic,
for the advent to come;
for I wash with water only
but he, with the sun!

THIRD VOICE

Who is it runs to the espousals
under a solar sign of mourning,
sackcloth clothed with coronas?
under a lunar tapestry of blood?

who but the unfortunate bridegroom
the hanged man dangling in the vault,
inverted in the sanguinary mirror,
untimely, under Pisces in the sea?

FIRST VOICE

Gaze upon the constellation
rising, Cetus, typhonic, shocked
into basalt by the gorgon-glance,
with howls in his throat, thrashing
the sea, heaved into a frenzy
to founder if he may, the luckless
mariner's embattled boat.

So give to the monstrous grave
this reluctant prophet, to his tomb
the bridegroom, under the roots
and bars of the rocks, in a mountainous
womb of the sea, bury him deep.

His threnody wails in the wild
wind, while darkness consumes
the sun; naught else avails but death
to render life back to the living.

Weigh if you can, astrologer
outwitted, how myth and mysterium
mingle, how manna remains
while chaff blows away.

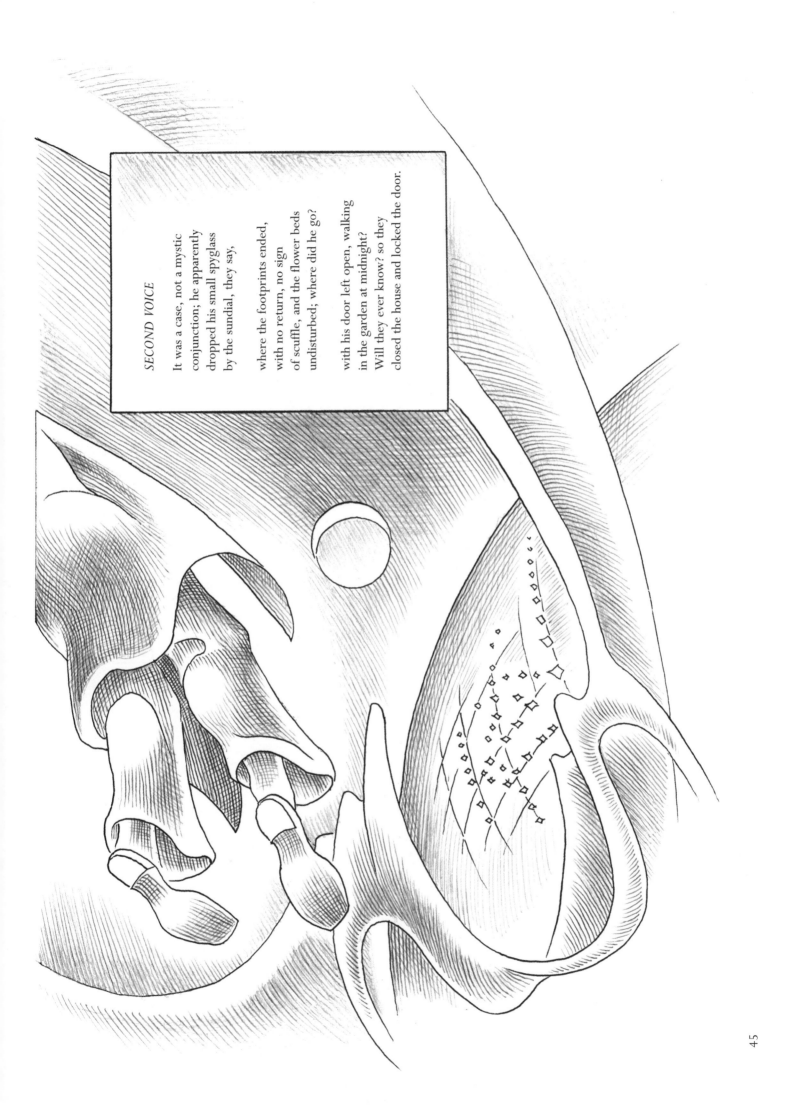

SECOND VOICE

It was a case, not a mystic
conjunction; he apparently
dropped his small spyglass
by the sundial, they say,

where the footprints ended,
with no return, no sign
of scuffle, and the flower beds
undisturbed; where did he go?

with his door left open, walking
in the garden at midnight?
Will they ever know? so they
closed the house and locked the door.

In diminishing air
we become his breath, his respiration,
lest in a bloody exudation
he succumb to terror

as stars rush down
in meteoric showers, and familiar
constellations wander in disarray
no longer circling Polaris.

SECOND VOICE

For you,
with a jewelled blue
earth-honed needle of light
lost in the stack of galactic darkness,
would say, wouldn't you,
how shall we ever, pray, navigate home?

we alone have heard your
terrified doubts, your wordless

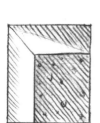
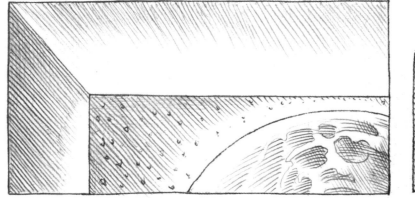

He was gone for a very long time.
When I follow the ranked
multitude of stars, as Ptolemy said,
my feet touch earth no longer.

THIRD VOICE

We are witness to the rapture
when the spirit seized him
like Habakkuk of old,
to his cry like a startled bird.

We heard the falling glass,
the cold thin rushing wind
of earth plummeting, her town
lamps dwindling below.

When the firmament drops
her blue-haloed veil, the aureole
of earth's curvature
bends like a bow.

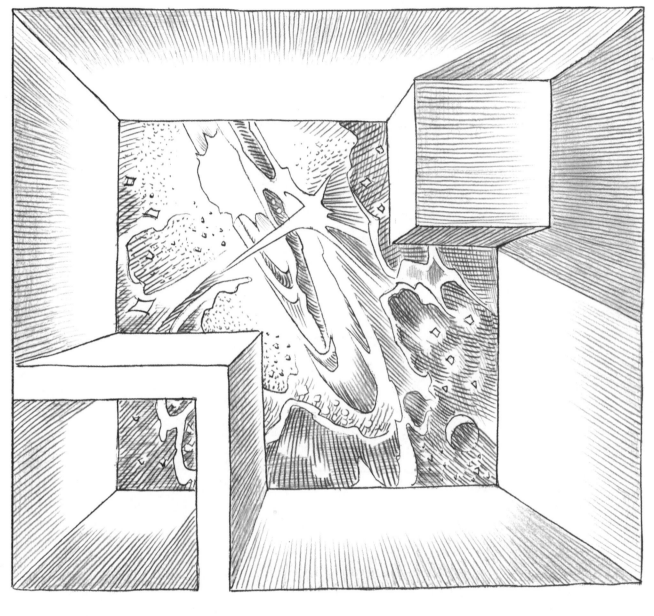

fears, have cast them out, for the dark
seas you are sailing, gleam
with watchfires, are signalled
with a host of lighthouses!

Emigrate, O traveller, beyond
the gossamer wake of the grandly
turning, the nebulous luminescence
one hundred thousand light years
wide, wheeling upon
its ponderous fiery axle,

where the galaxy's heart
in Sagittarius was all but engulfed,
remember? save glimmering skirts
milkily trailing their way
through cosmic thunderheads
to the hidden hub.

FIRST VOICE

So stand, my child, as a man

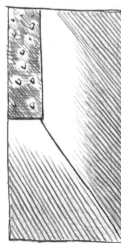

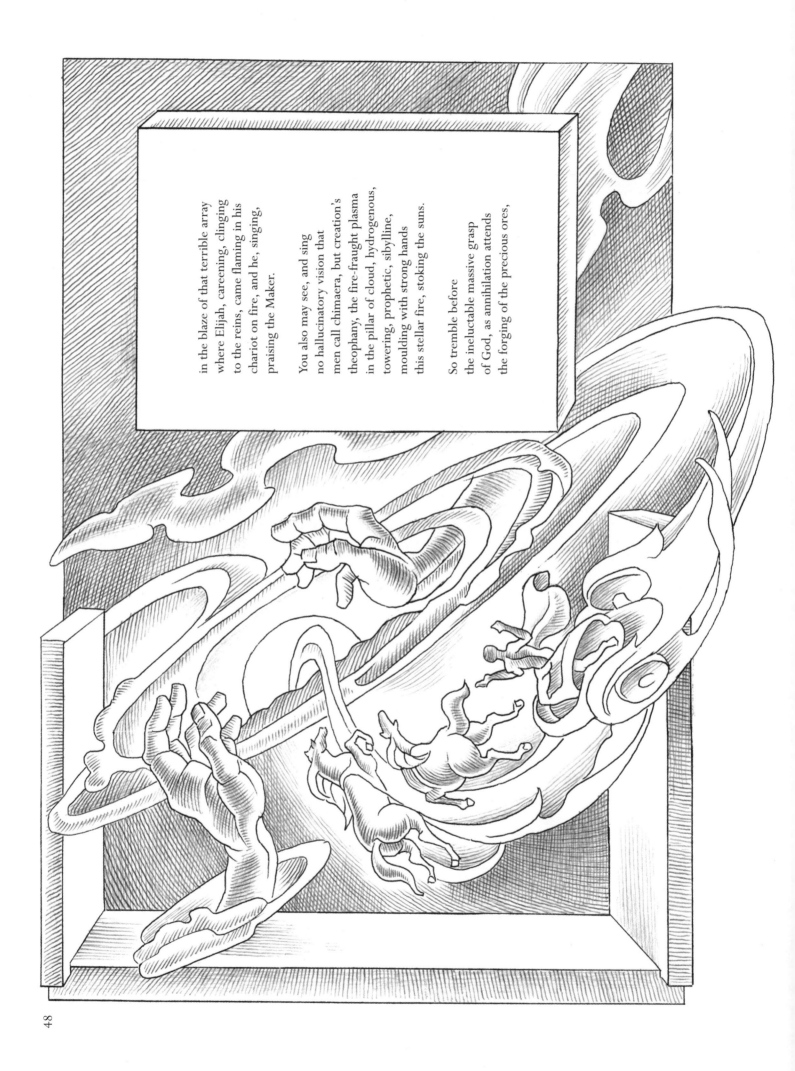

in the blaze of that terrible array
where Elijah, careening, clinging
to the reins, came flaming in his
chariot on fire, and he, singing,
praising the Maker.

You also may see, and sing
no hallucinatory vision that
men call chimaera, but creation's
theophany, the fire-fraught plasma
in the pillar of cloud, hydrogenous,
towering, prophetic, sibylline,
moulding with strong hands
this stellar fire, stoking the suns.

So tremble before
the ineluctable massive grasp
of God, as annihilation attends
the forging of the precious ores,

and beware the nuclear nova's collapse
where cracked, the catastrophic
solar egg falls in upon
its flaming ash,

SECOND VOICE

helium out of hydrogen
fusing, and oxygen for breathing
in the dew-forming sea-making rain
coalescing from carbon fueling
the growing of trees, with nitrogen
and luminous phosphorous
weaving genetic tapestries,

rare neon, magnesium,
crystalline silicon, the jeweller
and the builder calcium, architect
of bones and elegant shells,

rust-hued iron and iodine
for blood, fissionable
uranium with its deathwish,
and the gleaming, rustless,
malleable gold.

THIRD VOICE

So Phoenix reborn
thus claps with a roar of explosive
shock-blue plumage, her
scarlet, her green-gold grace
with wings unfurled and wafted
over the sea of space, she rains
dowries on the daughter of waters,
blue heavens over the new earth.

and though asleep is yet aware
of his carrier, the shoulder
his head lolls upon,
even as it dreams.

So out of oblivion,
borne on the wings of the penumbral
wind, I am wafted, quietly
to a slumbrous song

of the murmuring sea;
does earth reach out to receive,
her scented arms to caress me?
this sharp salt ocean air?

this warm sweet draught
of hayfields, of rose gardens?
under a paling sky at the first
bird-stirring light?

Yet beware of the ruined
crucible, this dervish sun
that whirls to a staggering death,
its mantle thrown, a carapace
of iron the panting heart constricts
till it bursts the vulcan face
in a last red fiery rush,

Charybdis! that ripped the vortex
sea apart, swallowing down
collapsing fire like foam
in a maelstrom; beware O child
of the frail sails, this balefire fall
of luciferian light, this reckless
slide into deep night
down into darkness.

THE MOURNER

Like a child falling asleep
at the fireworks, who is
bundled up in his father's arms
to be carried home.

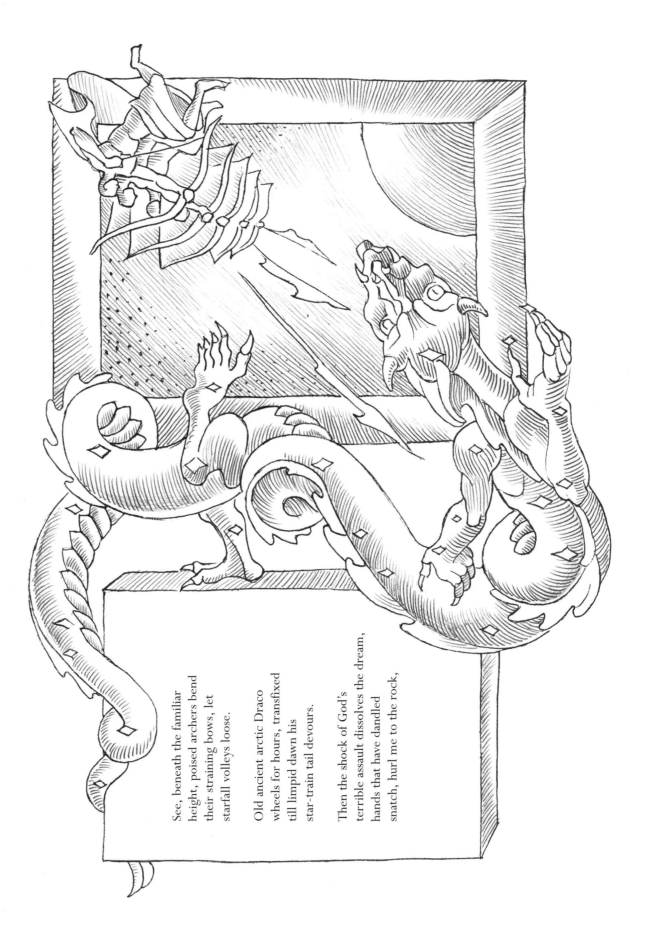

See, beneath the familiar
height, poised archers bend
their straining bows, let
starfall volleys loose.

Old ancient arctic Draco
wheels for hours, transfixed
till limpid dawn his
star-train tail devours.

Then the shock of God's
terrible assault dissolves the dream,
hands that have dandled
snatch, hurl me to the rock,

to the stone-paved plain,
batter me with light shafts
fired with a lion's roar, forged
in the furnaces of night,

while cratered, the grating
calamitous moon rolls over us,
an appalling thunderous tombstone
down, over the sky,

a blinding nemesis,
this ruby thin rapier probe
draws howls of a demoniac, his
Fall on us! Cover us!

rebound with a mountainous
mockery from the tomb:
Fall on us! Cover us!
O mountains of the moon!

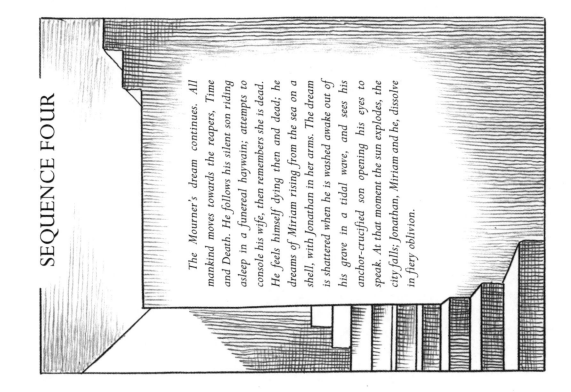

SEQUENCE FOUR

The Mourner's dream continues. All mankind moves towards the reapers, Time and Death. He follows his silent son riding asleep in a funereal haywain; attempts to console his wife, then remembers she is dead. He feels himself dying then and dead; he dreams of Miriam rising from the sea on a shell, with Jonathan in her arms. The dream is shattered when he is washed awake out of his grave in a tidal wave, and sees his anchor-crucified son opening his eyes to speak. At that moment the sun explodes, the city falls; Jonathan, Miriam and he, dissolve in fiery oblivion.

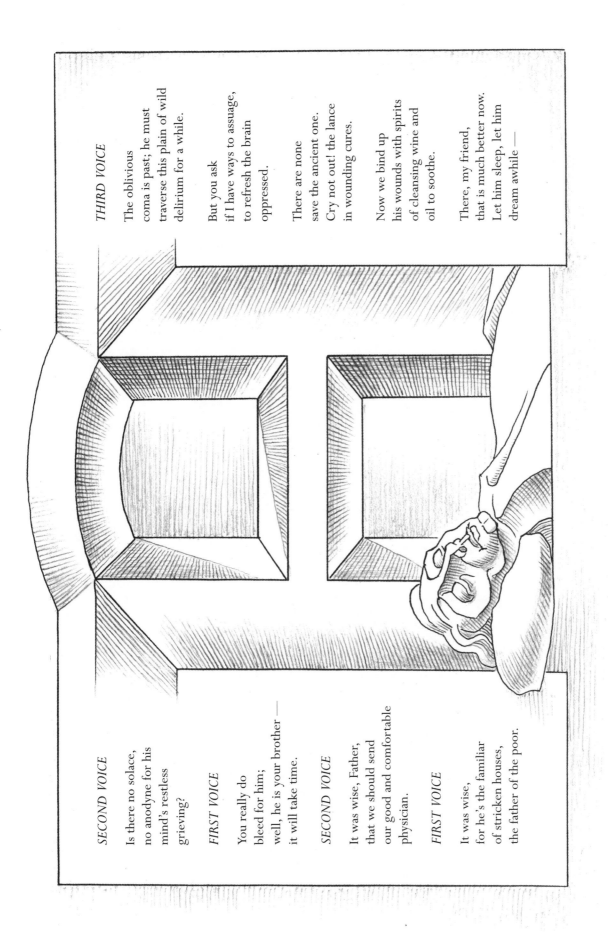

SECOND VOICE

Is there no solace,
no anodyne for his
mind's restless
grieving?

FIRST VOICE

You really do
bleed for him;
well, he is your brother —
it will take time.

SECOND VOICE

It was wise, Father,
that we should send
our good and comfortable
physician.

FIRST VOICE

It was wise,
for he's the familiar
of stricken houses,
the father of the poor.

THIRD VOICE

The oblivious
coma is past; he must
traverse this plain of wild
delirium for a while.

But you ask
if I have ways to assuage,
to refresh the brain
oppressed.

There are none
save the ancient one.
Cry not out! the lance
in wounding cures.

Now we bind up
his wounds with spirits
of cleansing wine and
oil to soothe.

There, my friend,
that is much better now.
Let him sleep, let him
dream awhile —

55

SECOND VOICE

Pulvis protoplasti
Semen sic humatum,
Solis aqua et sanguine
Coelicola est factum.

Sown earth-born dust
Of Adam's earth,
Each by the waters
And the sun's blood
Is Heaven's heir —

FIRST VOICE

Crepuscular dusk,
this imperceptible waning of daylight,
like an old man's fading sight,
diminishes, almost unnoticed,
till there's none.

And you are there
with your startled eyes,
fearful, listening, as if to apprehend
some shadow in darkness,
some looming death walk

of refugees, with the old
wagons creaking under household
loads of bedding and baggage,
with the children crying,
riding into exile.

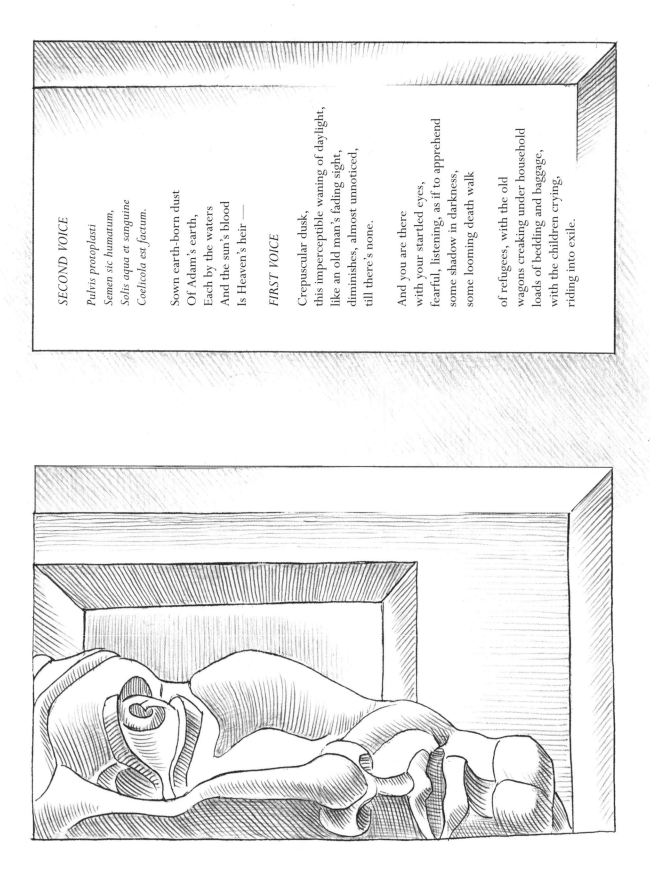

56

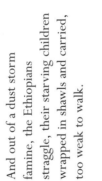

And out of a dust storm
famine, the Ethiopians
straggle, their starving children
wrapped in shawls and carried,
too weak to walk.

What manner of
stumbling procession this? a ceaseless
shuffling of countless feet
limping, bleeding and shoeless,
over the flintlike plain?

Such is man's ferocity,
more terrible than plague;
these murderous midnight marches
of humankind as cattle
to unspeakable extinction!

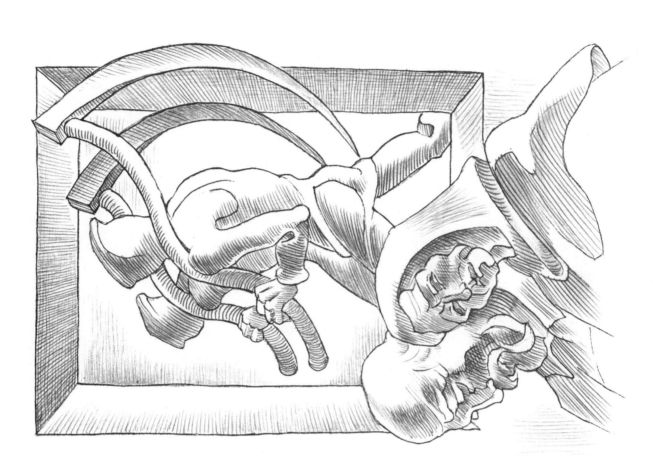

THIRD VOICE

And even as Joshua's
sun stood still and the moon
in the valley of Aijalon,
so time consumes its midnight now,
harvests the afternoon.

Though slow or sudden, Time
and Death, these are the Reapers then;
they wade into the golden fields
unshouldering, honed to a mortal edge,
their curving scythes

fall to the funereal
mowing, their swung blades
fatal pendulums, descend
on the rout of the old heads
ripe for toppling into rows.

Old legs like stems
shatter, even the young and the green,
as if machine-gunned from under them;
so lilies lie with thistles strewn,
weeds with the wheat.

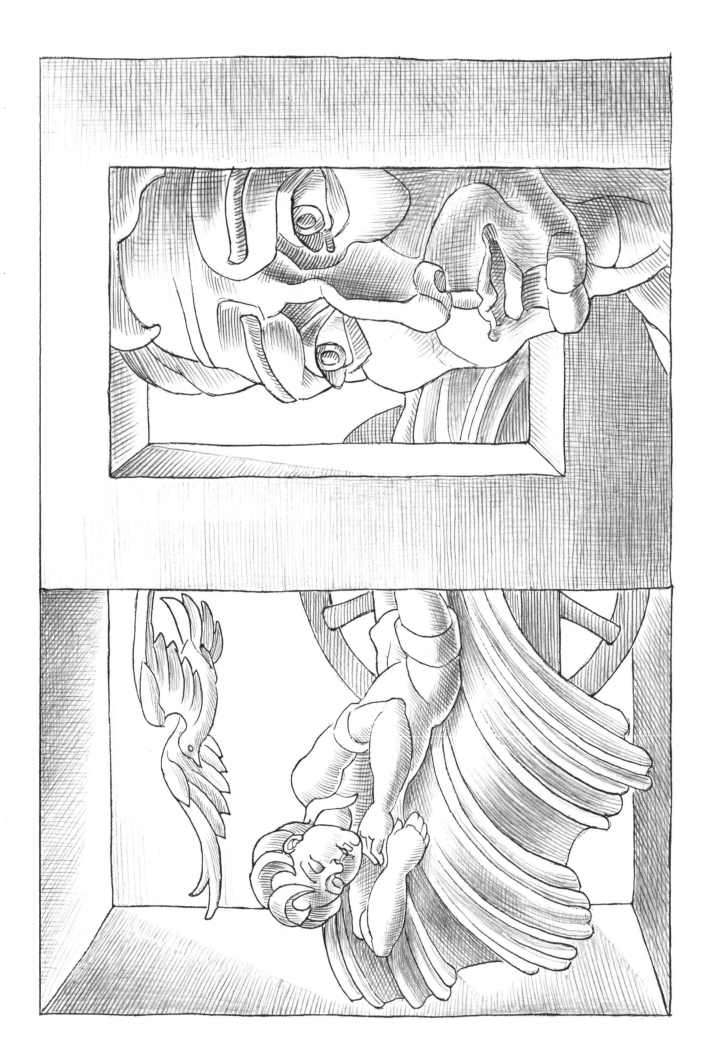

SECOND VOICE

Even the strongest
manhandling sheaves,
are they not dying and even now
dead? are they not burying
their own dead as sown
seed, to be reaped again?

Even the child riding high
under the clouds, reclining
in a midsummer nest like a bird
in a dream, will he startle and sing?
thy son, old father, riding
this haywagon home?

THE MOURNER

Not now, he will not
stir now; I fear for him.
He may not even hear
the trumpeting wind

when that day comes;
he may not even see,
being blind, the sky rolled up
in a scroll of fire,

or heed, poor scholar
so often late for school,
with none then to rouse him
in that ominous hour

unknown to men;
when will it be, by sundown
tomorrow? or a hundred thousand
harvests hence?

and where will he find
his frail remains, poor waif
orphaned and bereft of sense
and of the living breath?

Gone into the golden
haze, his smiling face lingers
like a sundog, a haloed rainbow
on the circle of the sun

called parhelion,
sleeping, dreaming still
and fading as a rainbow
when the rain moves on.

Do not weep, my poor
Miriam, our small son
like a stunned sparrow after a storm
has been carried home.

Why do you hold
your eyes closed, dear soul,
so sorrowful when I console you?
and you cannot look at me,

you cannot even hear
when I am close and whisper;
you remain a stone, remote from me,
pitiful effigy.

SECOND VOICE

Even stone is eroded
by the frost and the rain
and the river to a handful of sand
ferried to the sea, even granite,
to a fistful of clay.

In your arms you embrace
the chilled beloved, the translucent
ghost of a glacier that recedes
blue, with the echoes of her
milky dissolution.

FIRST VOICE

Oh, trouble him no longer
with the ache of his arms
around empty illusion; her
face is grown fading, cavernous,
away, so bloodless, and wasted
with wind and rain.

In a squall of sudden
grief, he is weak, a toppled
headstone rolled back on sod;

the sweat breaks cold on his face
as dew does on graveyard
marble or slate.

SECOND VOICE

Lethargic, he sprawls,
leaden of tongue, his buckled
feet and knees numb already;
he cannot speak or recall
the beloved ghost gone now over seas,
his pulseless blood crawls
in his limbs, comes cold
into his heart, congeals —

Death it seems is a secret
curative, a medicine for all ills;
the convalescent takes the air
with a view to the sea, his
ultimate sanitarium a hillside
cemetery, where the seasons
snow him asleep under blossoms,

maple fall, snowfall, rainfall
and the sun again, as the tender
grass grows over him.

64

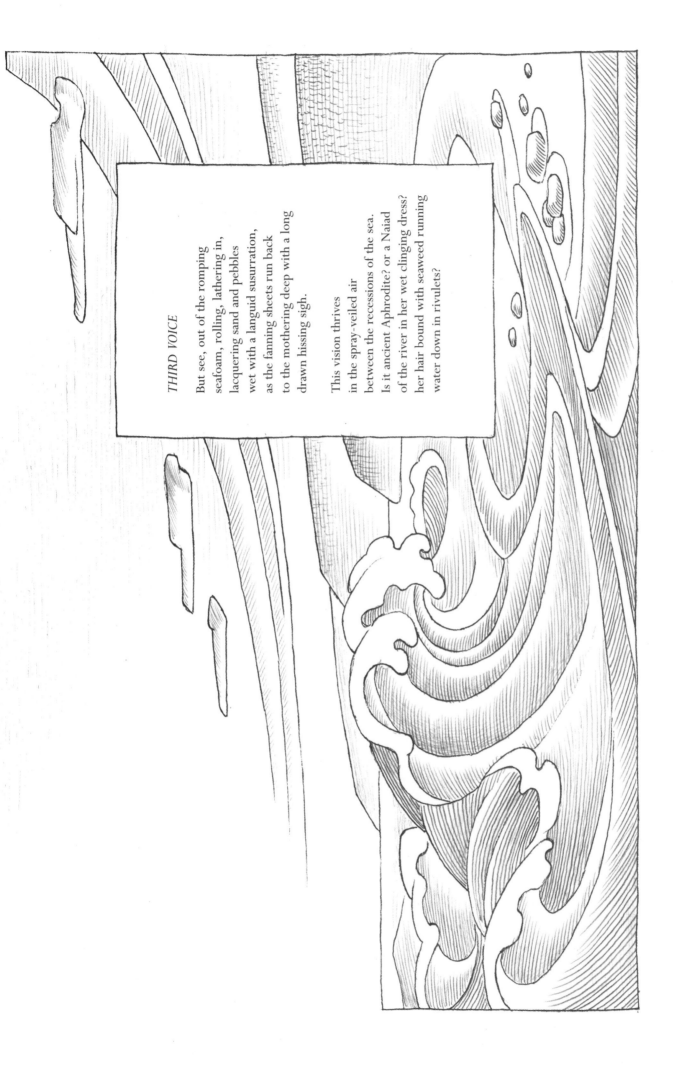

THIRD VOICE

But see, out of the romping
seafoam, rolling, lathering in,
lacquering sand and pebbles
wet with a languid susurration,
as the fanning sheets run back
to the mothering deep with a long
drawn hissing sigh.

This vision thrives
in the spray-veiled air
between the recessions of the sea.
Is it ancient Aphrodite? or a Naiad
of the river in her wet clinging dress?
her hair bound with seaweed running
water down in rivulets?

For she rides the cockleshell,
fondling Jonathan in his
boyhood grace, lifted from the dark
and deepest garden where he lay;
Miriam it is who weeps
at the cold boy's limp arms
escaping her embrace.

See, the mounting wave's
glimmering glass-green wall of water
when the cresting cave, trembling,
embowers her, till she, beyond
hearing, the moment seeming
hours, as the foam-veil
falls, disappears.

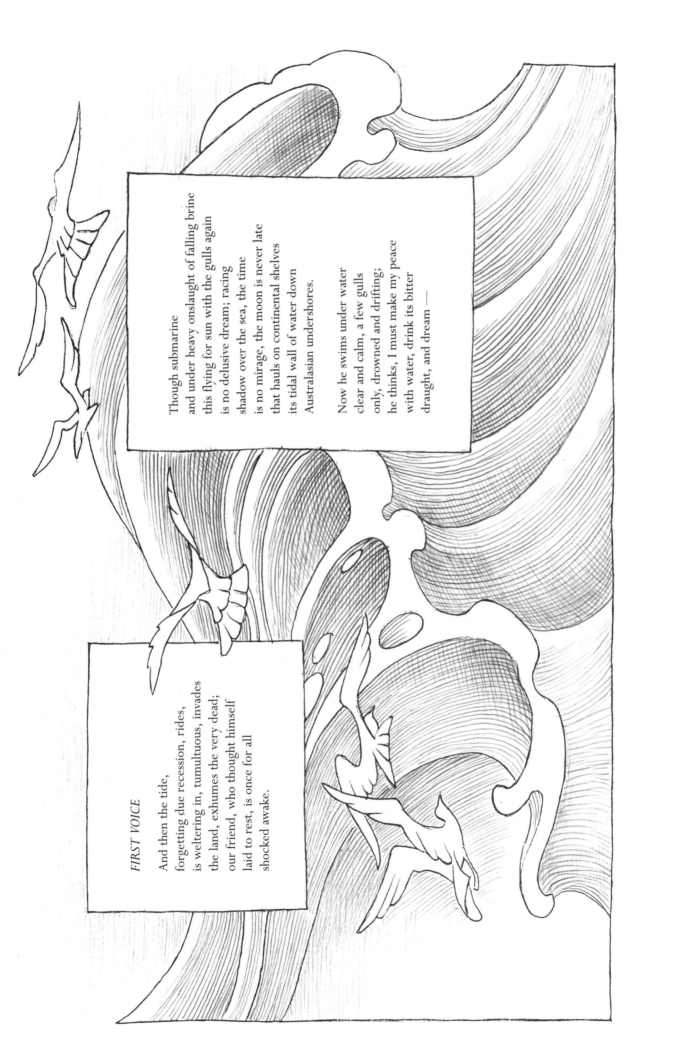

Though submarine
and under heavy onslaught of falling brine
this flying for sun with the gulls again
is no delusive dream; racing
shadow over the sea, the time
is no mirage, the moon is never late
that hauls on continental shelves
its tidal wall of water down
Australasian undershores.

Now he swims under water
clear and calm, a few gulls
only, drowned and drifting;
he thinks, I must make my peace
with water, drink its bitter
draught, and dream —

FIRST VOICE

And then the tide,
forgetting due recession, rides,
is weltering in, tumultuous, invades
the land, exhumes the very dead;
our friend, who thought himself
laid to rest, is once for all
shocked awake.

SECOND VOICE

The ocean seems a round
of amniotic crystal, shot through
with sun, with a crimson streaming stain
spiraling down, thinks he, gathering me
in the wake of a sign, bleeding
into the sea stream.

Could it be a great iron hook
through a silver scaled fish? an anchor
perhaps, with a dolphin impaled?
or Phaethon the unfortunate, fallen?
No, no Ichthys, no dolphin,
no Icarus, marbled

in the shimmering sea,
but a silvery child with his hands
riveted to the stock, an anchor it is!
his feet transfixed to the shank, his
pierced side gashed by the fluke that
raked him from the sea-floor!

Dear God! is it
you, Jonathan? the draught
he's draining stifles the cry. But he
sees not pain's opacity, nor the glazed
stare of death. When the child's eyes
open, they are clear!

What joy, when the child's
lips part, like a silver sanctus
bell of treble voice; 'Seek not the living,
father, among the dead; He is not here—
he has risen as he said.'

THE MOURNER

What happened then
I do not well remember — some
vast explosion of the sea, a steaming
concourse of erupting cloud,

of floating aerial debris.
I saw somehow, screened in mist
the sun's unfolding fireball
engulf the very sky.

And now, in this after
darkness, I know not why
or how I came to be standing, dazed,
in that deadly street.

I watched, benumbed,
the silent shock wave come.
It raced through seeming stillness
beyond the speed of sound.

I could not run; the buildings
began to buckle and collapse;
sudden seismic chasms opened
their howling devastations.

When the wind struck
I saw her, the child was hurled away.
As Lot's wife became salt, she stumbled
in Sodom, writhing in fire!

72

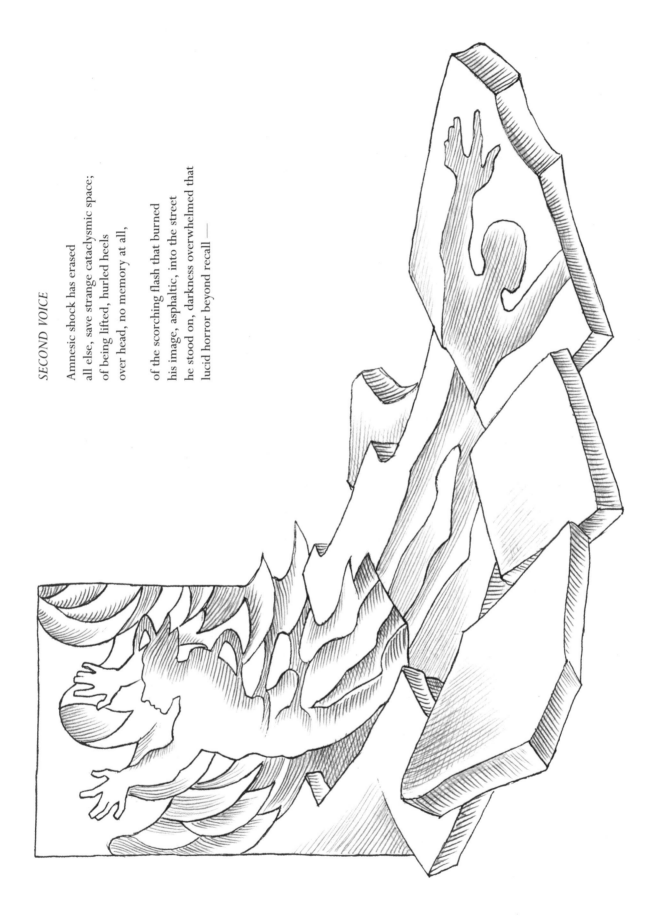

SECOND VOICE

Amnesic shock has erased
all else, save strange cataclysmic space;
of being lifted, hurled heels
over head, no memory at all,

of the scorching flash that burned
his image, asphaltic, into the street
he stood on, darkness overwhelmed that
lucid horror beyond recall —

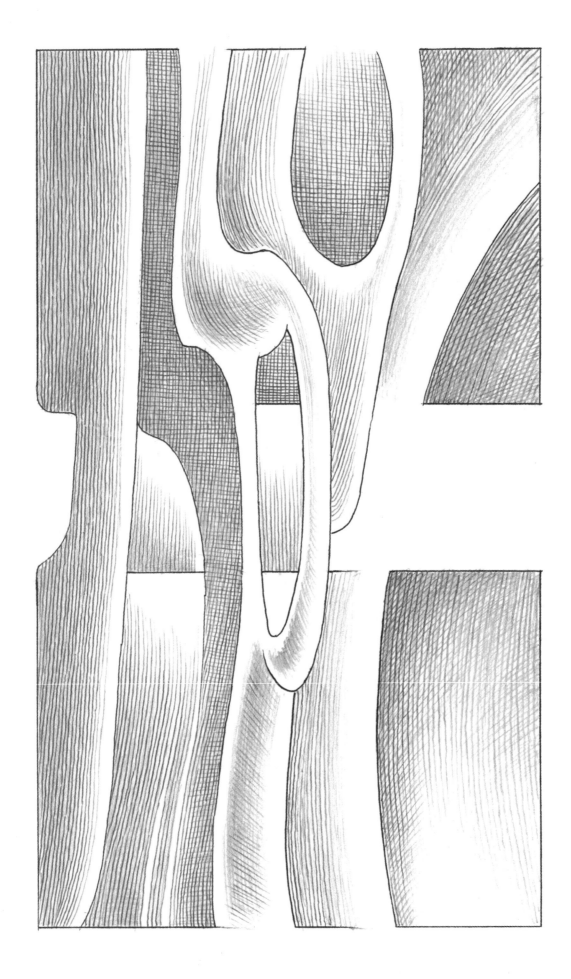

SEQUENCE FIVE

The world as we know it has ended; total darkness, total silence, total death, and yet he awakes, hearing the trumpets of the last day. He discovers himself disembodied, and strangely begins to hope. Though the world is a cemetery and the sea a desert, seven angels stride over it, trumpeting. The earthquake of resurrection begins. Bones are gathered and rise as the Prophet foretold. Under the moon like a death's head, he descends again into the underworld, but his son is no longer there. He comes up, wildly searching among the dead, when suddenly he sees his own skeleton, moves toward it as all the dead begin murmuring 'immutabimur!' — we shall be changed! He enters the house of his bones, and, as dawn breaks, begins the risen life.

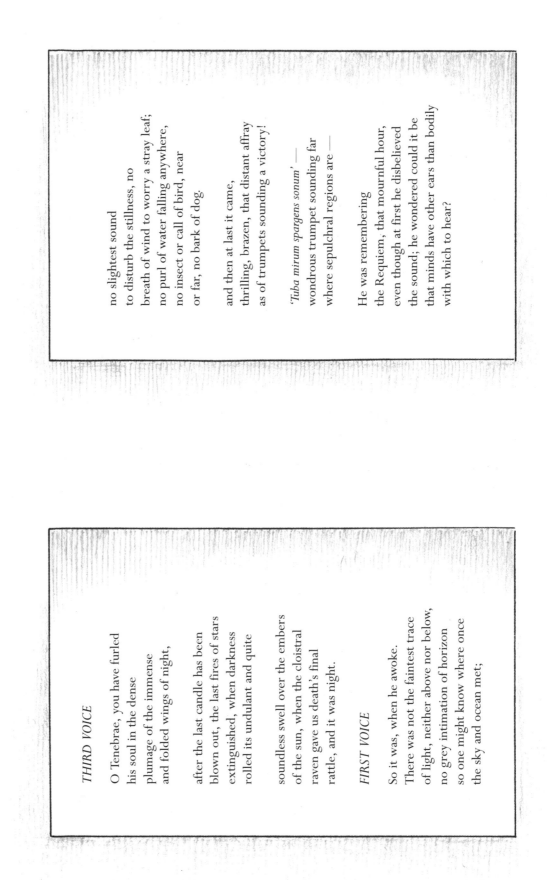

no slightest sound
to disturb the stillness, no
breath of wind to worry a stray leaf;
no purl of water falling anywhere,
no insect or call of bird, near
or far, no bark of dog.

and then at last it came,
thrilling, brazen, that distant affray
as of trumpets sounding a victory!

'Tuba mirum spargens sonum' —
wondrous trumpet sounding far
where sepulchral regions are —

He was remembering
the Requiem, that mournful hour,
even though at first he disbelieved
the sound; he wondered could it be
that minds have other ears than bodily
with which to hear?

THIRD VOICE

O Tenebrae, you have furled
his soul in the dense
plumage of the immense
and folded wings of night,

after the last candle has been
blown out, the last fires of stars
extinguished, when darkness
rolled its undulant and quite

soundless swell over the embers
of the sun, when the cloistral
raven gave us death's final
rattle, and it was night.

FIRST VOICE

So it was, when he awoke.
There was not the faintest trace
of light, neither above nor below,
no grey intimation of horizon
so one might know where once
the sky and ocean met;

THIRD VOICE

He strayed, unthinking
with his hand, as if to catch
the clear reverberant echoes dying,
and found, almost without dismay
and strangely unshaken, that there was
no ear — nor a hand to cup the ear!

Nor were the intangible
fingers an obstacle to vision,
for even as darkness waned in a pale
prelusion of dawn, his hand could not
shield him from the sight or shock
of ruinous desolation.

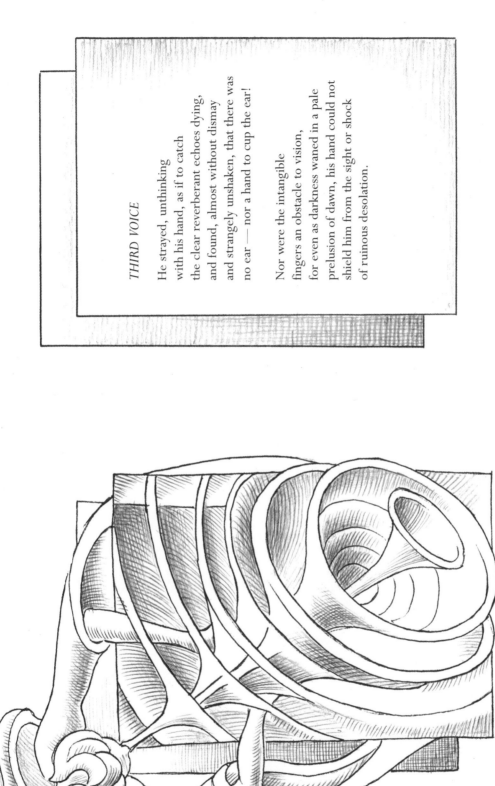

He seemed to go through
all the motions of his body
in the mind, without stirring a muscle;
panic and sick fright should have
surged in him, yet calmly alert
he grappled with the inconceivable

that there was no head!
an eyeless, faceless distillation only,
no neck or chest or limbs — unless,
quite invisible, hovering over a scorched
hieroglyph, whose he could not
remember — could it be?

78

FIRST VOICE

A fragment of the corner
of his house still stood, an empty
doorway leading nowhere, bricks
fused into glass, stones burned
into powder, the cemetery's old wall
was fallen, shattered, its burial
grounds entombed in ash.

the toppled grave cross
leans in a dune of windblown sand;
no remnants anywhere to show
that trees had ever grown there,
only a skeleton strewn in cinders,
the cynical skull rolled apart,
bleached a wind-scoured white.

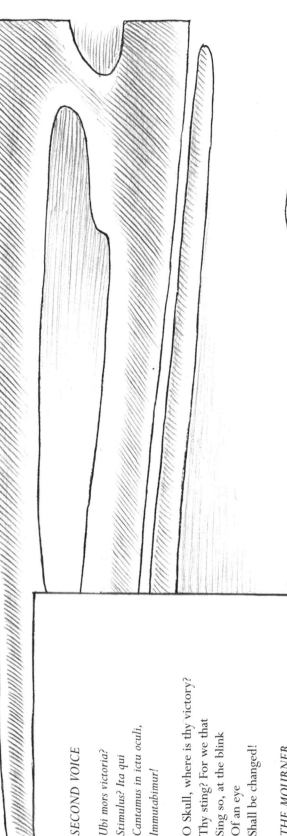

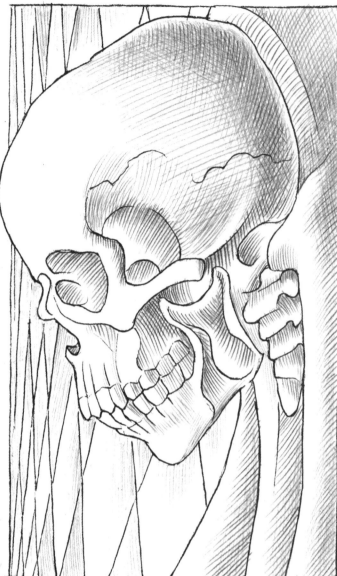

SECOND VOICE

Ubi mors victoria?
Stimulus? Ita qui
Cantamus in ictu oculi,
Immutabimur!

O Skull, where is thy victory?
Thy sting? For we that
Sing so, at the blink
Of an eye
Shall be changed!

THE MOURNER

I seem to remember the priest
chanting, and my friend with his words
as if one were the other, standing here
when they buried my son.

Yet words said once were
spoken now, were even heard;
'what kind of victory can death have?'
do spirits hear the truth of sound?

will this skull here
who has no eyes to terrify,
ever fear death again? will he obey
commands, who has no ears to hear?

Entirely, an earthly population
lies under the untrodden graves.
Why the inscriptions should have been cut,
almost all indecipherable now,
quite weathered away, is hard saying;
perhaps the dying slaves

who engraved them were driven
to forestall that last remorseless hour,
when the iron bones of ruined buildings
would prod their distant tells, looming
volcanic, like intrusions, outcroppings
eroded from later sedimentation.

And beyond this strictly human
degradation, the lordly sea retreats
by slow degrees down sloping shales
the wind whips, in a waterless waste
fraught with piratic gold and broken
ships, and the bones of whales.

nothing more to lose,
no desires to be bribed; he cannot
be stung by whips or threats. He is death's
trophy of insolent indifference.

Perhaps others, immaterial
as I, that I cannot see, hover here
who have fled the abode of death and are
free at last — there may be hope.

FIRST VOICE

When lifted into clear
air, his spirit sees, it seems,
a cemetery some cyclopean architect
laid out to the horizon, endless
as death, a vast public pavement
of granite gravestones.

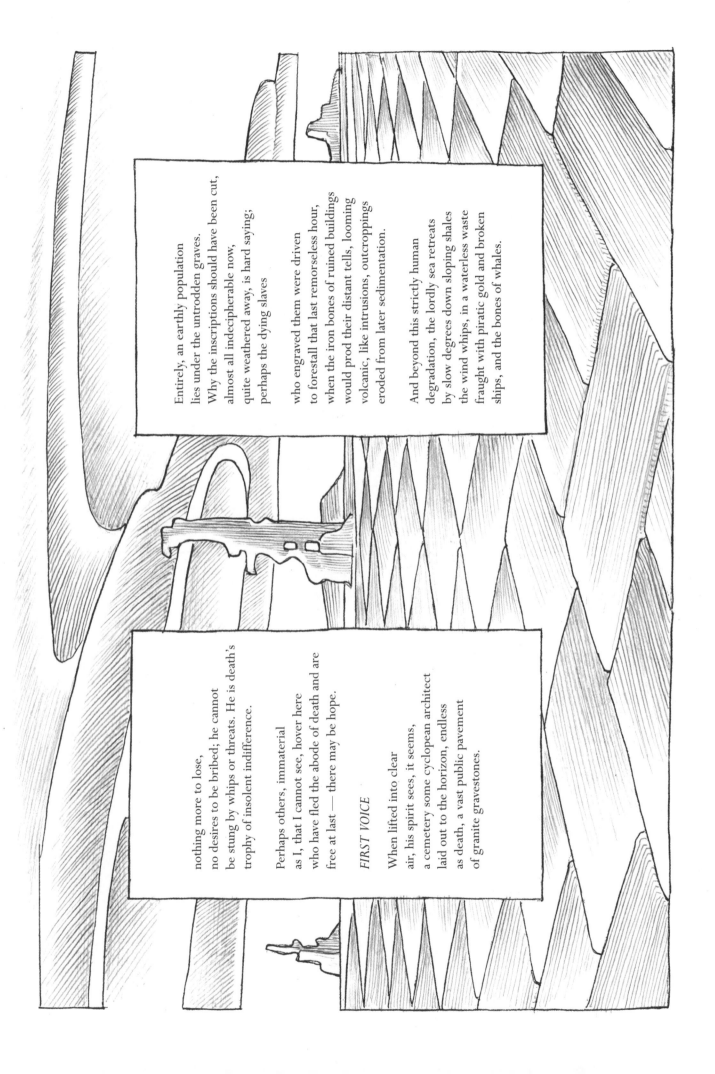

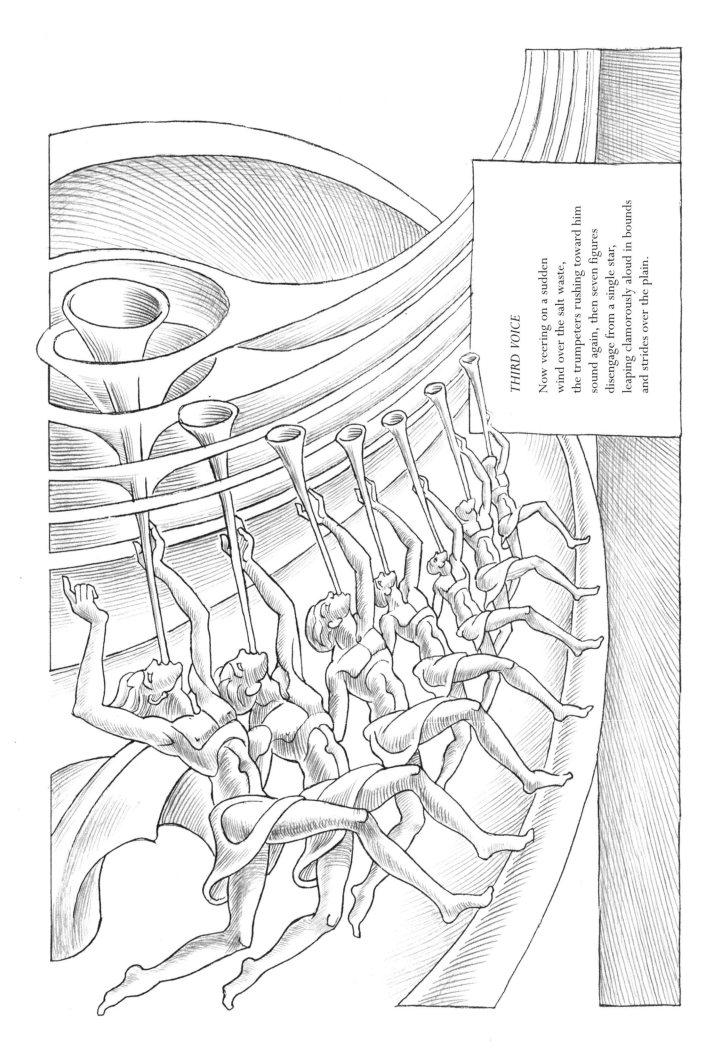

THIRD VOICE

Now veering on a sudden
wind over the salt waste,
the trumpeters rushing toward him
sound again, then seven figures
disengage from a single star,
leaping clamorously aloud in bounds
and strides over the plain.

82

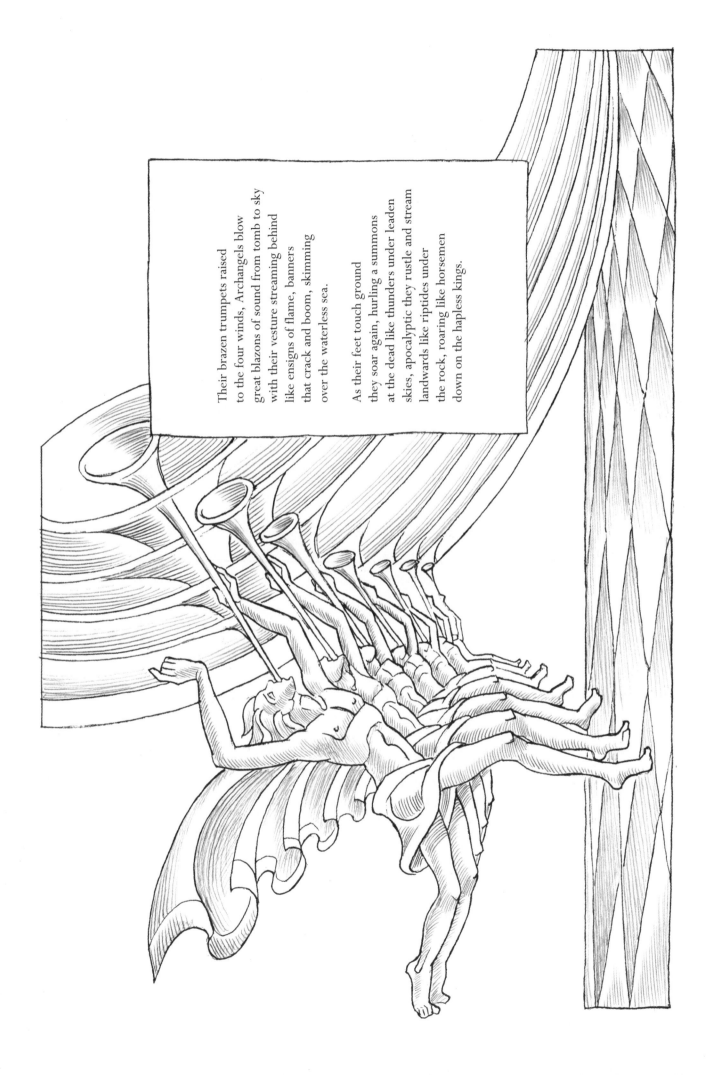

Their brazen trumpets raised
to the four winds, Archangels blow
great blazons of sound from tomb to sky
with their vesture streaming behind
like ensigns of flame, banners
that crack and boom, skimming
over the waterless sea.

As their feet touch ground
they soar again, hurling a summons
at the dead like thunders under leaden
skies, apocalyptic they rustle and stream
landwards like riptides under
the rock, roaring like horsemen
down on the hapless kings.

FIRST VOICE

So the plain begins to quake
and tremble with a tearing tectonic
growl under ground as earth-plates
rise and shift, slide and fall, like
ice floes breaking on a river thaw,
or a wind-rolled rising of the sea,
so granite buckles and rides,

begins to expose under rising
rock the grave-darkness crouching within
while skeletal, a thin hand grasps
an edge as if it might haul itself
back to life, but the shifting
gravestone falls; the severed phalanges
roll away, delicate as spools.

THIRD VOICE

You are shaken with emotion
remembered, as bones, shoulder and arm,
purchase a precarious leverage,
appear to be raising on scapula
splintered, this fragile assemblage
unconscious of pain, to be shouldering
back, its graven memorial.

Another slab with a clatter
upends, and a woman long dead
sits up in her shroud; her veil,
disturbed by the air crumbles and
falls, ashes from bones, for the graves
open of their own accord, as if spirits
were thieves, exhuming the dead.

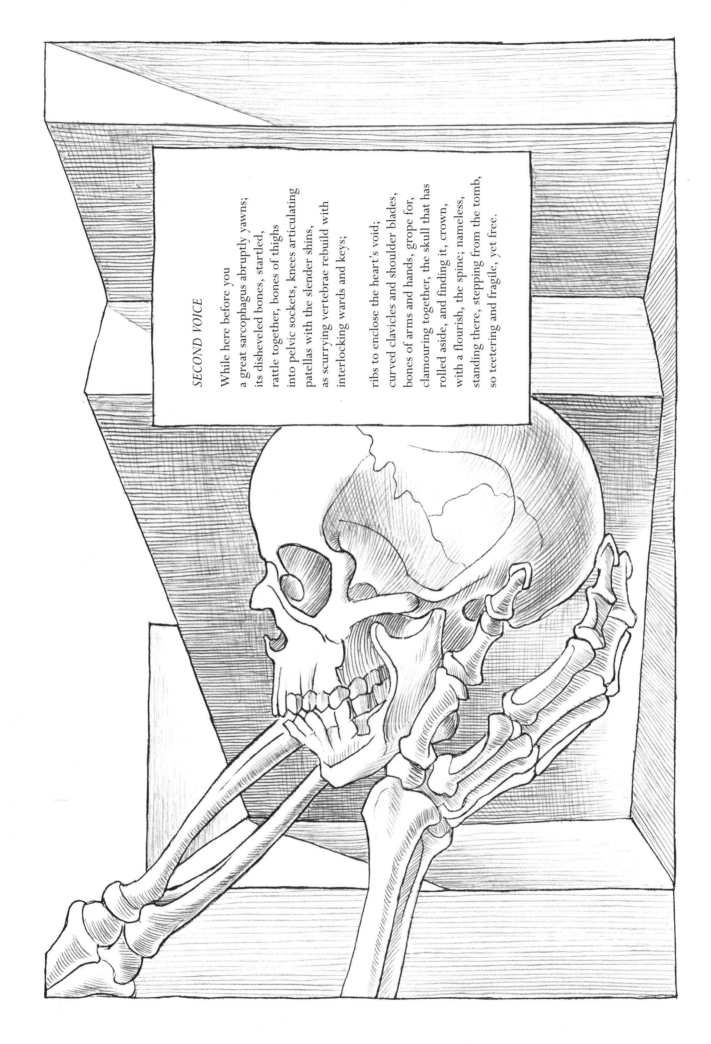

SECOND VOICE

While here before you
a great sarcophagus abruptly yawns;
its disheveled bones, startled,
rattle together, bones of thighs
into pelvic sockets, knees articulating
patellas with the slender shins,
as scurrying vertebrae rebuild with
interlocking wards and keys;

ribs to enclose the heart's void;
curved clavicles and shoulder blades,
bones of arms and hands, grope for,
clamouring together, the skull that has
rolled aside, and finding it, crown,
with a flourish, the spine; nameless,
standing there, stepping from the tomb,
so teetering and fragile, yet free.

THIRD VOICE

And the word of the Lord
came to Ezekiel, saying:

O my people,
I will open your graves
and have you rise from them,
and bring you back
to the land of Israel.

Then you shall know
that I am the Lord, when I
open your graves, and have you
rise from them,
O my people.

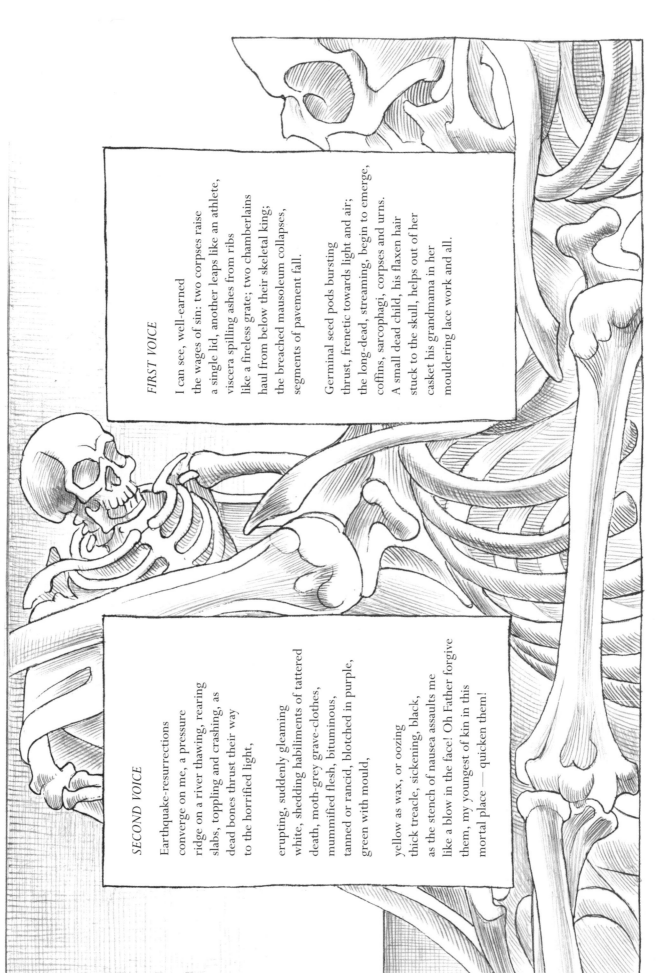

FIRST VOICE

I can see, well-earned
the wages of sin: two corpses raise
a single lid, another leaps like an athlete,
viscera spilling ashes from ribs
like a fireless grate; two chamberlains
haul from below their skeletal king;
the breached mausoleum collapses,
segments of pavement fall.

Germinal seed pods bursting
thrust, frenetic towards light and air;
the long-dead, streaming, begin to emerge,
coffins, sarcophagi, corpses and urns.
A small dead child, his flaxen hair
stuck to the skull, helps out of her
casket his grandmama in her
mouldering lace work and all.

SECOND VOICE

Earthquake-resurrections
converge on me, a pressure
ridge on a river thawing, rearing
slabs, toppling and crashing, as
dead bones thrust their way
to the horrified light,

erupting, suddenly gleaming
white, shedding habiliments of tattered
death, moth-grey grave-clothes,
mummified flesh, bituminous,
tanned or rancid, blotched in purple,
green with mould,

yellow as wax, or oozing
thick treacle, sickening, black,
as the stench of nausea assaults me
like a blow in the face! Oh Father forgive
them, my youngest of kin in this
mortal place — quicken them!

SECOND VOICE

Listen, child of Adam, you will hear the great seven angels approaching, their lightening foot-falls in waves of shock rebounding over the wasteland.

FIRST VOICE

Their height seems taller, like colossi, as they come, towering more vastly in their span of straddling seas, and awful under their vaulted soaring.

SECOND VOICE

Their limbs, burnished, gleam in the light strayed under earth's curve coming, running up on the trumpets raised, jubilant in peals, rinsing skies awake.

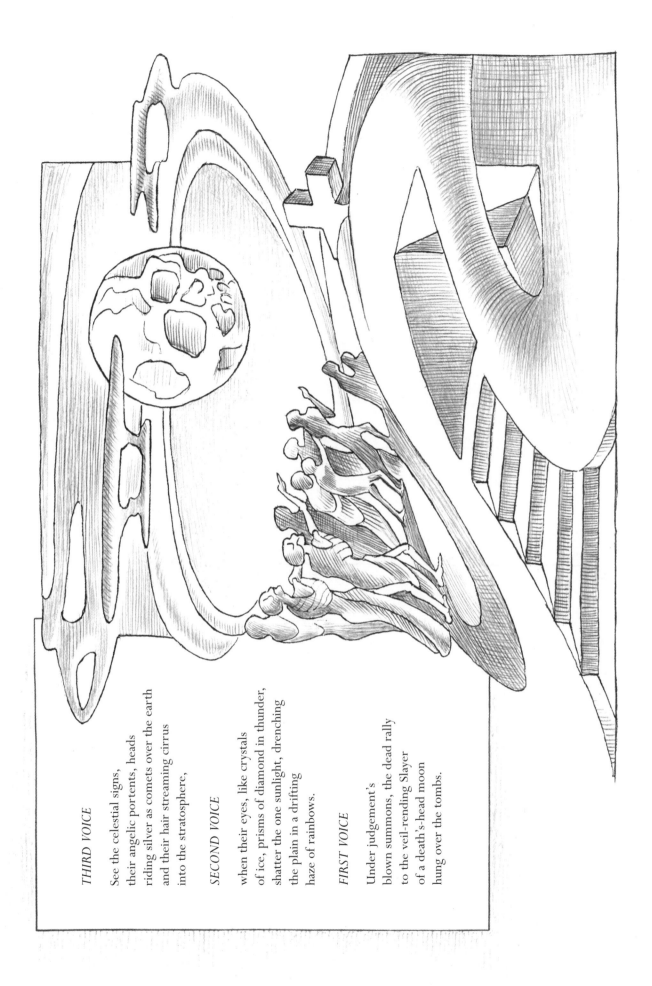

THIRD VOICE

See the celestial signs,
their angelic portents, heads
riding silver as comets over the earth
and their hair streaming cirrus
into the stratosphere,

SECOND VOICE

when their eyes, like crystals
of ice, prisms of diamond in thunder,
shatter the one sunlight, drenching
the plain in a drifting
haze of rainbows.

FIRST VOICE

Under judgement's
blown summons, the dead rally
to the veil-rending Slayer
of a death's-head moon
hung over the tombs.

THIRD VOICE

And you resume descent
where it began before
among stone hewn mausolea
and tombs, remember?
searching for a son? stumbling
up steps on a sarcophagus
abandoned by the boy,
and you seek him
down the corridor of death's
doorway, now devoid of him.

If ghosts could weep
you should have wept by now,
alone, abandoned underground,
by clamorous bones
and coffins receding
in a rout of sound.

THE MOURNER

Is it time sliding into one?
do I see the future still to come?
remembering it as if it were
what has been, and is done?

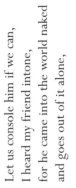

Let us console him if we can,
I heard my friend intone,
for he came into the world naked
and goes out of it alone,

divested of his flesh and blood.
Let us clothe him in repentance,
another voice replied, my life
in him was loving wife and child.

My soul wept for tears, then,
the drippings of the cave,
as the hood fell holy over me
a benison for pain,

a billowing stole over
bodiless feet that flew
from solitude there, to meeting him
in the upper air —

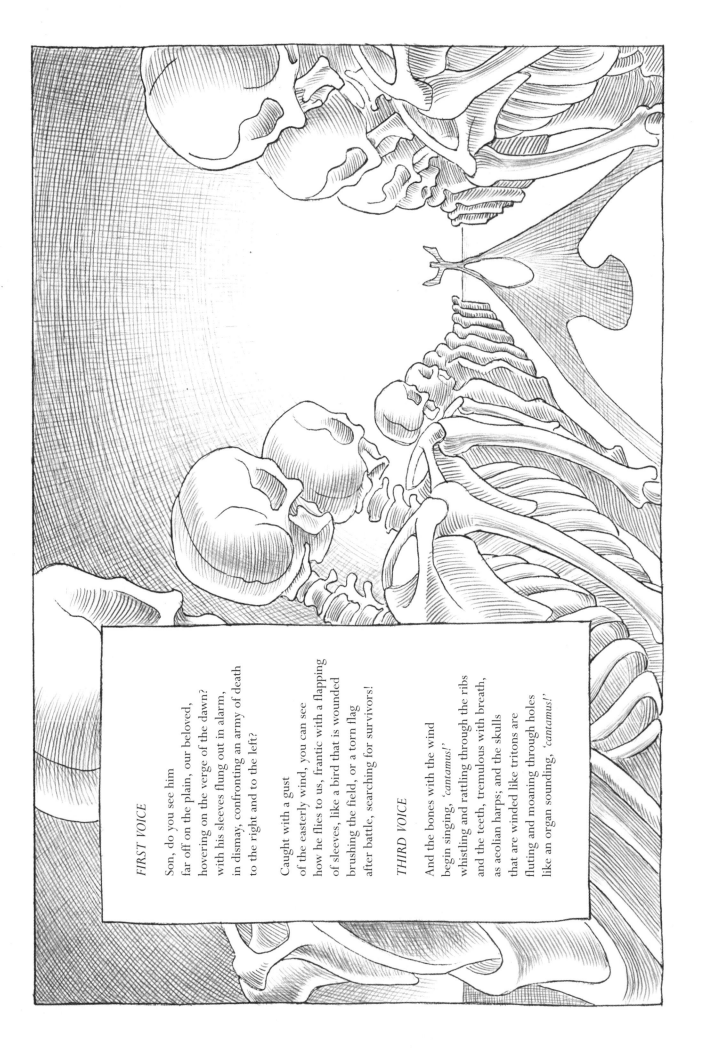

FIRST VOICE

Son, do you see him
far off on the plain, our beloved,
hovering on the verge of the dawn?
with his sleeves flung out in alarm,
in dismay, confronting an army of death
to the right and to the left?

Caught with a gust
of the easterly wind, you can see
how he flies to us, frantic with a flapping
of sleeves, like a bird that is wounded
brushing the field, or a torn flag
after battle, searching for survivors!

THIRD VOICE

And the bones with the wind
begin singing, *'cantamus!'*
whistling and rattling through the ribs
and the teeth, tremulous with breath,
as aeolian harps; and the skulls
that are winded like tritons are
fluting and moaning through holes
like an organ sounding, *'cantamus!'*

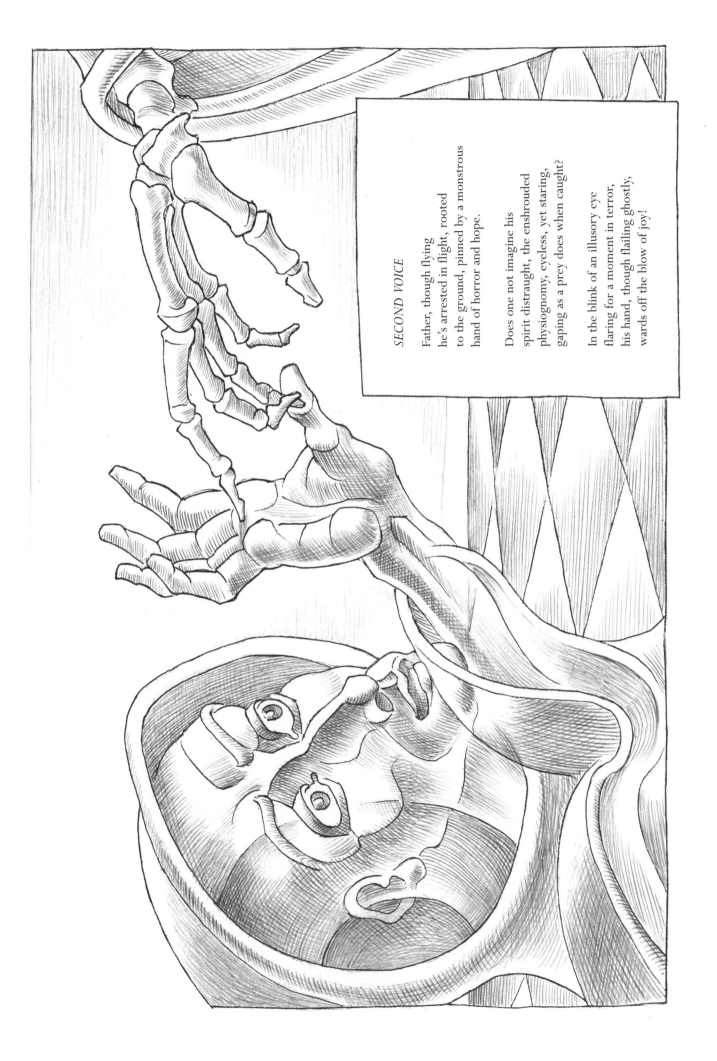

SECOND VOICE

Father, though flying
he's arrested in flight, rooted
to the ground, pinned by a monstrous
hand of horror and hope.

Does one not imagine his
spirit distraught, the enshrouded
physiognomy, eyeless, yet staring,
gaping as a prey does when caught?

In the blink of an illusory eye
flaring for a moment in terror,
his hand, though flailing ghostly,
wards off the blow of joy!

THE MOURNER

I saw it then, my house
of bones, my own skeleton
standing, not alone
but in the ranks of the west.

And the sea broke then
and returned to the bay
in a thunder of spray, where it
flew on the freshening wind,

washing all dust, all
corruption away, as I westerly
glide from the robe of my mourning
and escape like a sigh,

like a sylph out of sleeves,
like a flowering scent
of verdure, a vernal
rustling of leaves.

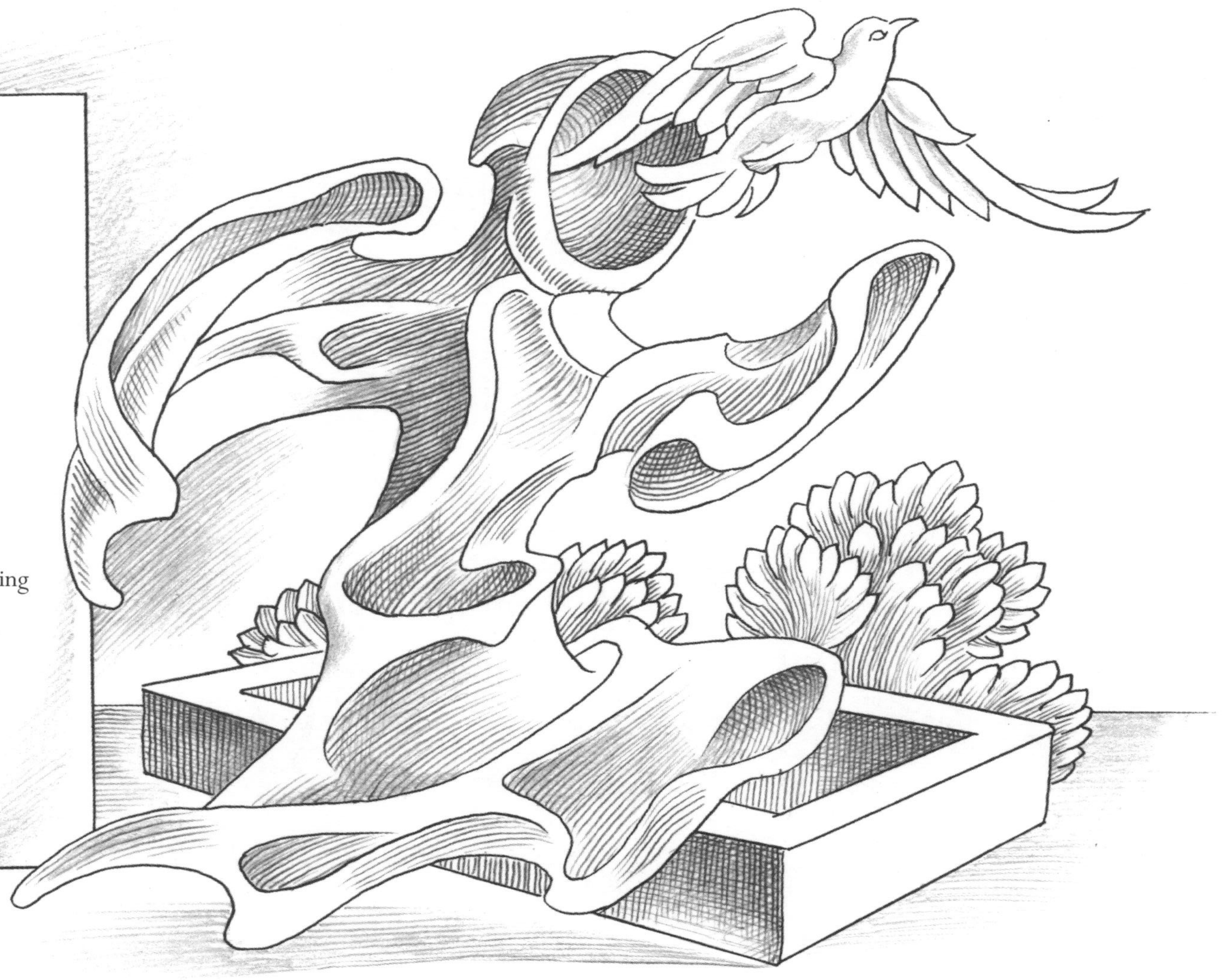

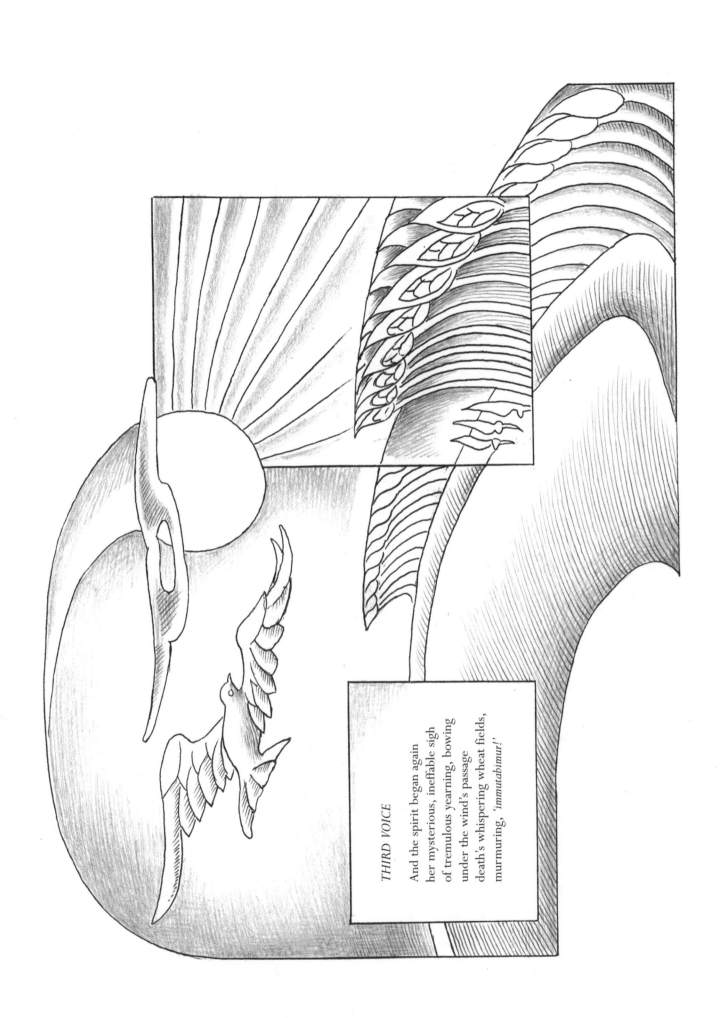

THIRD VOICE

And the spirit began again
her mysterious, ineffable sigh
of tremulous yearning, bowing
under the wind's passage
death's whispering wheat fields,
murmuring, *'immutabimur!'*

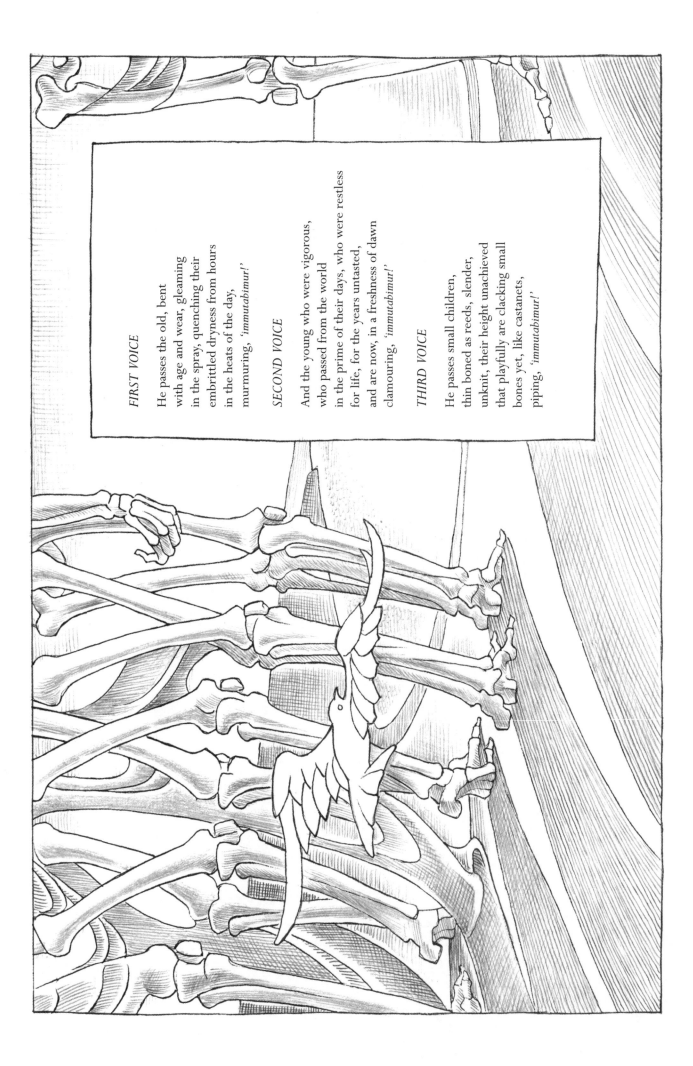

FIRST VOICE

He passes the old, bent
with age and wear, gleaming
in the spray, quenching their
embrittled dryness from hours
in the heats of the day,
murmuring, '*immutabimur!*'

SECOND VOICE

And the young who were vigorous,
who passed from the world
in the prime of their days, who were restless
for life, for the years untasted,
and are now, in a freshness of dawn
clamouring, '*immutabimur!*'

THIRD VOICE

He passes small children,
thin boned as reeds, slender,
unknit, their height unachieved
that playfully are clacking small
bones yet, like castanets,
piping, '*immutabimur!*'

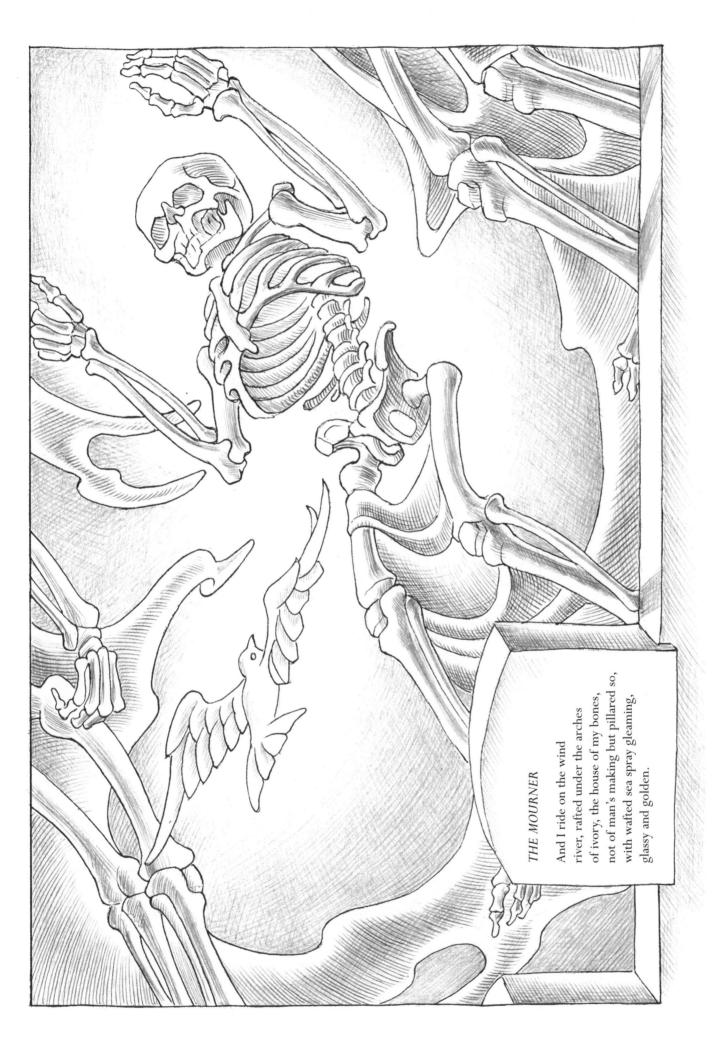

THE MOURNER

And I ride on the wind
river, rafted under the arches
of ivory, the house of my bones,
not of man's making but pillared so,
with wafted sea spray gleaming,
glassy and golden.

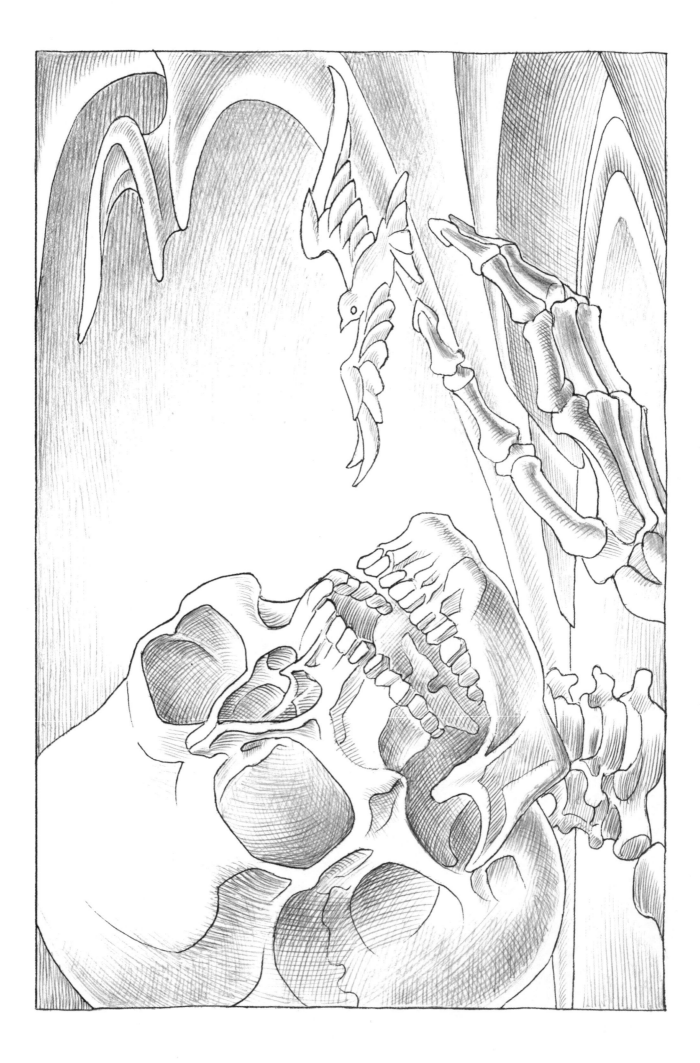

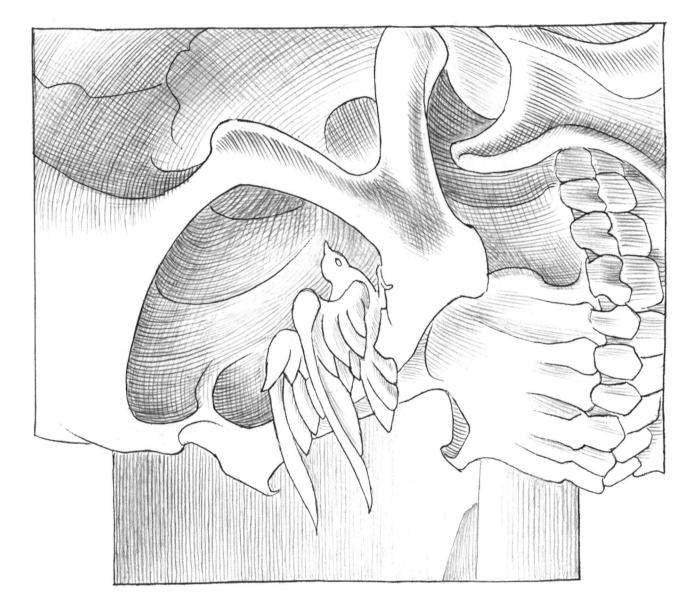

I'm hushed as I enter
under the frontal moulding,
of a brow's tympanum, lofty
and broad, under the orbital
vaulted porches, humbled
through optic apertures,

where the doubled nerves
brought single vision in,
so enter I, the cranial and dim
cave of the oracle of God,
and pray on the palatine step
of Bethesda's pool,

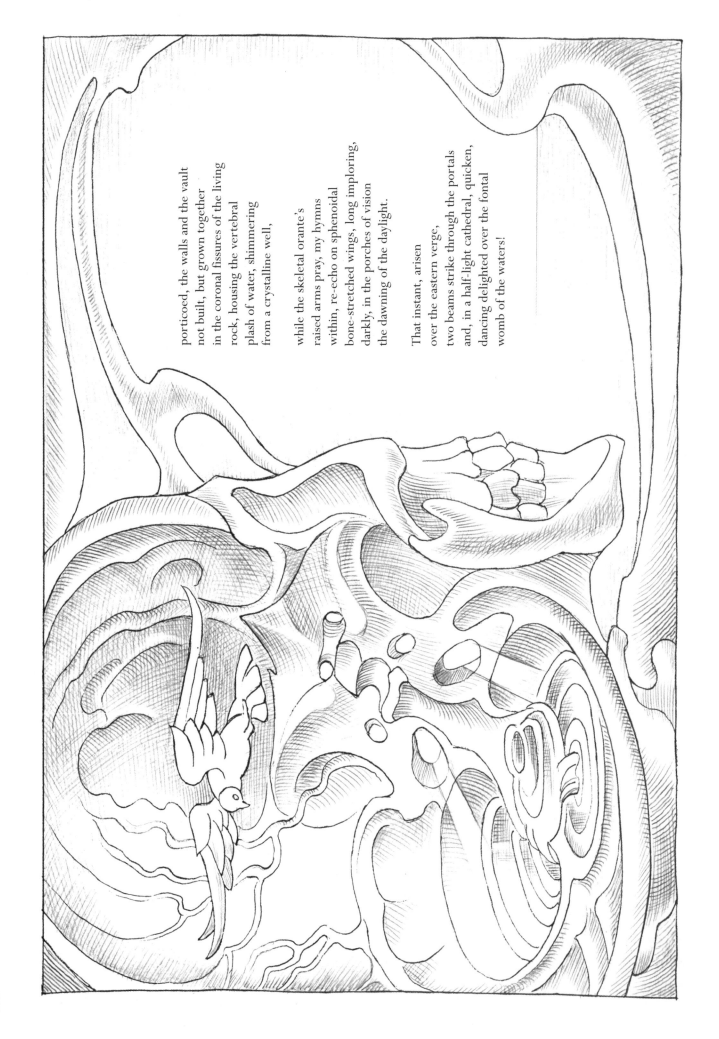

porticoed, the walls and the vault
not built, but grown together
in the coronal fissures of the living
rock, housing the vertebral
plash of water, shimmering
from a crystalline well,

while the skeletal orante's
raised arms pray, my hymns
within, re-echo on sphenoidal
bone-stretched wings, long imploring,
darkly, in the porches of vision
the dawning of the daylight.

That instant, arisen
over the eastern verge,
two beams strike through the portals
and, in a half-light cathedral, quicken,
dancing delighted over the fontal
womb of the waters!

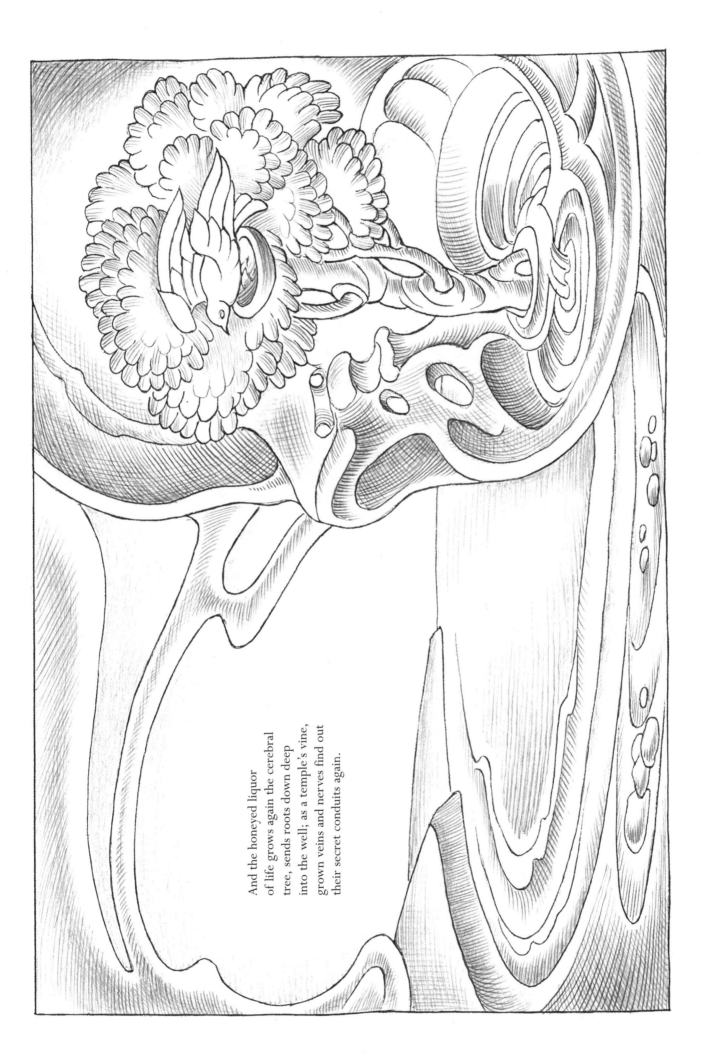

And the honeyed liquor of life grows again the cerebral tree, sends roots down deep into the well; as a temple's vine, grown veins and nerves find out their secret conduits again.

And the heart begins
beating in its costal cage, the blush
of its blood, like a rose, enclosed
in a garden pavilion, its fiery flood's
arterial ramblings bud and flower
in my flesh again.

Muscular ligaments,
tendons coalesce, draw over them
the delicate integument of sense,
spring nuances, coolness of dew, I'm
hearing again quite daft and enraptured
the din of the birds!

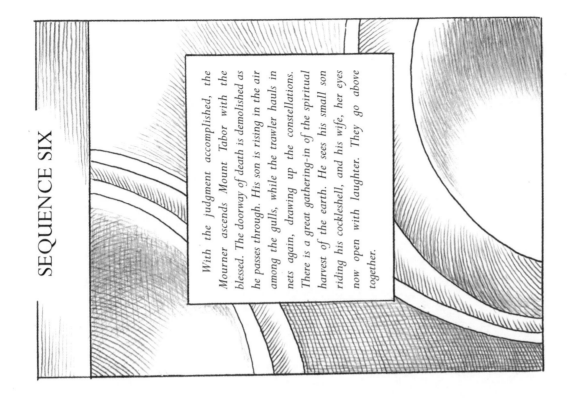

With the judgment accomplished, the Mourner ascends Mount Tabor with the blessed. The doorway of death is demolished as he passes through. His son is rising in the air among the gulls, while the trawler hauls in nets again, drawing up the constellations. There is a great gathering-in of the spiritual harvest of the earth. He sees his small son riding his cockleshell, and his wife, her eyes now open with laughter. They go above together.

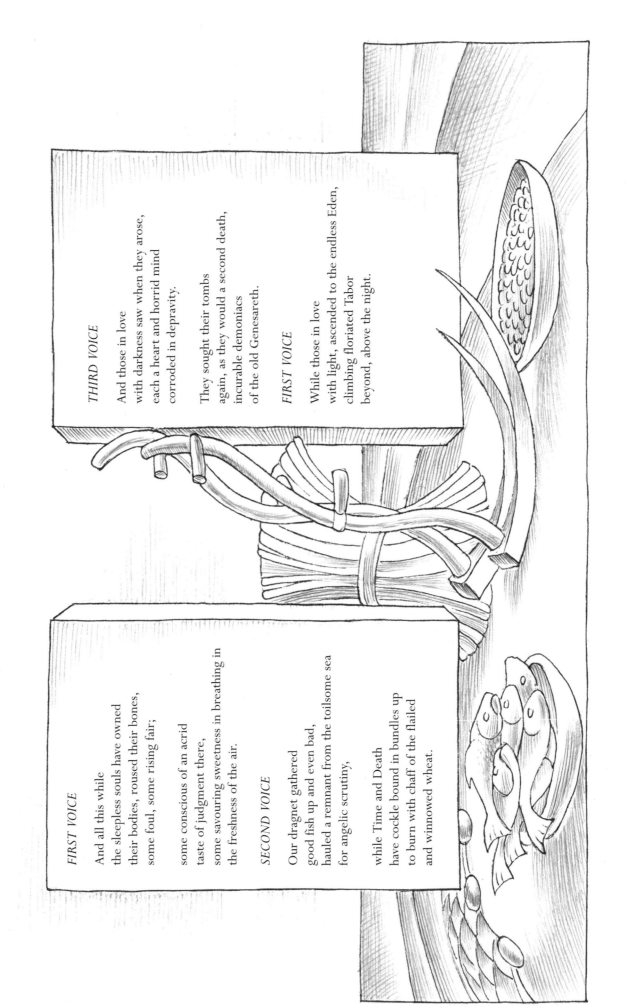

FIRST VOICE

And all this while
the sleepless souls have owned
their bodies, roused their bones,
some foul, some rising fair;

some conscious of an acrid
taste of judgment there,
some savouring sweetness in breathing in
the freshness of the air.

SECOND VOICE

Our dragnet gathered
good fish up and even bad,
hauled a remnant from the toilsome sea
for angelic scrutiny,

while Time and Death
have cockle bound in bundles up
to burn with chaff of the flailed
and winnowed wheat.

THIRD VOICE

And those in love
with darkness saw when they arose,
each a heart and horrid mind
corroded in depravity.

They sought their tombs
again, as they would a second death,
incurable demoniacs
of the old Genesareth.

FIRST VOICE

While those in love
with light, ascended to the endless Eden,
climbing floriated Tabor
beyond, above the night.

THE MOURNER

When I heard the singing larks
descanting on the canon or the fugue
of a million other musics,

I knew myself become
a changed and ageless youth,
where the past and future fuse

in song, the instant ages meld;
tomorrow is a thousand years ago,
while yesterday is even now today.

To speak of it, we need invent
a language more song than speech,
a vision more than meaning;

must hone the clouded metaphor
to adamantine precision,
faceting the diamond fire;

must clarify like melting ice
the density of words, the
hoar of the frosted trope.

If one could cope
with the divine hilarity of laughter
or the rushing stormless

sigh of pity, one might
gather like a blessed fool reaping
beatitudes of sorrow,

some inimitable language
one might hear, like the silken sighing
of boreal aurora.

And I began then to see,
as a man has never seen before,
the faces of his friends.

We had no need of speaking,
for all was true and understood
walking the amaranthine wood

like lanterns moving
luminous with moonlight phases,
waxing, waning at will

with inward smiling wisdom;
and we walked with the joy of children
in vales of asphodel.

FIRST VOICE

My people, almost weightless,
climb my holy mountain,
bounding over the heights, each
lightly as a gazelle.

Come my beloved one, my
friend there, quaffing as stags do
streams of tinkling ice-melt
under the mossed rocks.

THIRD VOICE

Come under the cool
shade of seracs hung in the blue-
green infinite of the alpine air,
where springtime blooms anew

with second summer's
pale hepaticas, snow-hued,
lavendered; golden cupped anemones
brimming with dew.

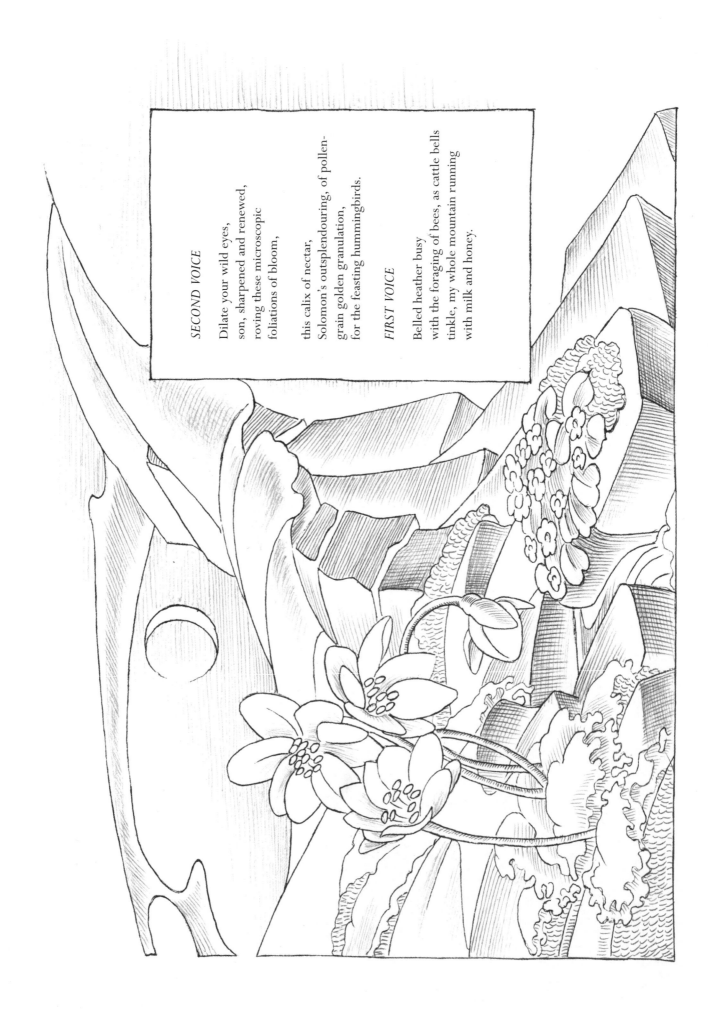

SECOND VOICE

Dilate your wild eyes,
son, sharpened and renewed,
roving these microscopic
foliations of bloom,

this calix of nectar,
Solomon's outsplendouring, of pollen-
grain golden granulation,
for the feasting hummingbirds.

FIRST VOICE

Belled heather busy
with the foraging of bees, as cattle bells
tinkle, my whole mountain running
with milk and honey.

THIRD VOICE

Come to espy the once
dead moon, its meteoric seas
a tranquillity of lakes, that
mirror this earthly Eden,

and the sun's undazzling
refulgence that blinds no eye
as it runs rejoicing, untented,
its fire-dance gigantic

FIRST VOICE

over the holiest of steps.
Enter my granite prostyle, threshold
doors opening, temporal, eternal,
to the illimitable Light!

THE MOURNER

And I saw in that noontide
splendor of lustrous halation
the shadow of my son,

playing in the light,
with a movement of enraptured
levitation like music,

trailing his long shadow-
sleeves, on tiptoes waiting
for the knowing shock

of a lifeless gateway
jettisoned in space, falling
away over the turning earth,

fourfold, of ponderous
granite split, fissured in a rumbling
demolition of death!

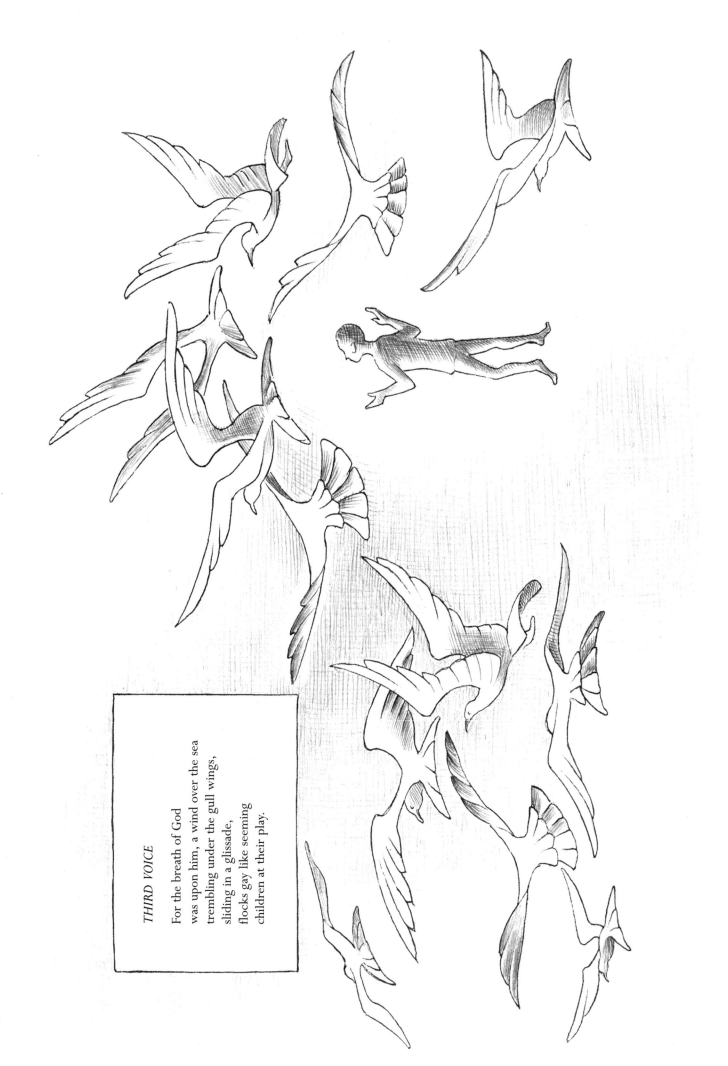

THIRD VOICE

For the breath of God
was upon him, a wind over the sea
trembling under the gull wings,
sliding in a glissade,
flocks gay like seeming
children at their play.

SECOND VOICE

You remember rising
under the mackerel-vaulted skies?
how, following the cosmic catch
that shattered, drawn up,
the refracted, shafted sun,
you broke into another air?
where a trawler hauled under its old
sail, nets flickering into a hold?

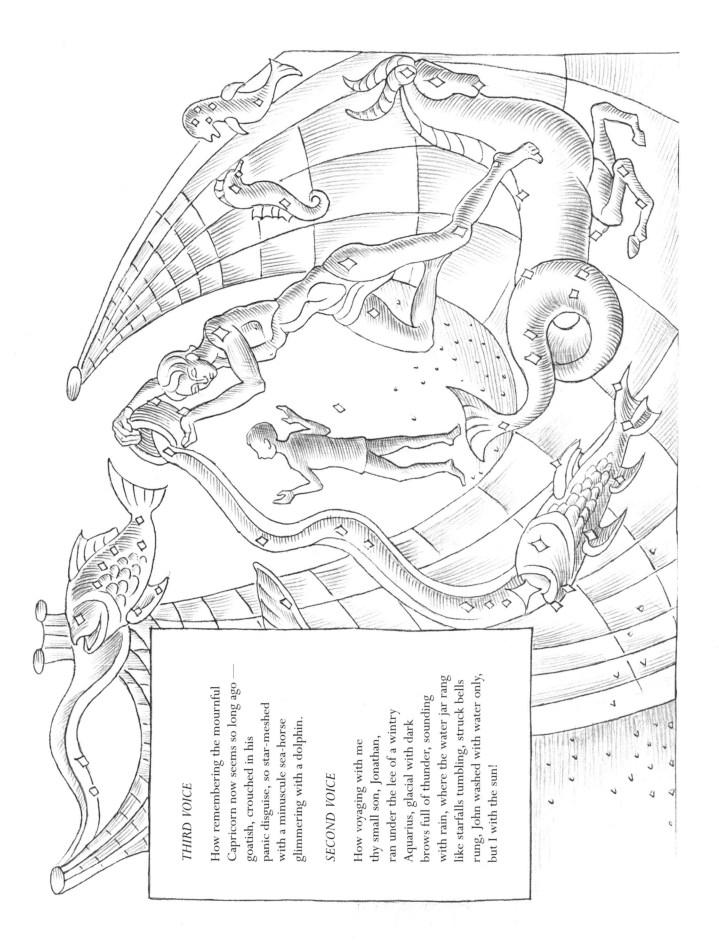

THIRD VOICE

How remembering the mournful
Capricorn now seems so long ago —
goatish, crouched in his
panic disguise, so star-meshed
with a minuscule sea-horse
glimmering with a dolphin.

SECOND VOICE

How voyaging with me
thy small son, Jonathan,
ran under the lee of a wintry
Aquarius, glacial with dark
brows full of thunder, sounding
with rain, where the water jar rang
like starfalls tumbling, struck bells
rung, John washed with water only,
but I with the sun!

THIRD VOICE

You remember, old father?
the prodigious arrival of Leviathan,
lunging in a resounding rush,
down out of a cloud of blown sea-
spray and air, raining to the surface,
shivering up in showers?

FIRST VOICE

Was it not he? Cetus, typhonic?
with howls in his throat, thrashing
the sea heaved into a frenzy
to founder, if he might, the luckless
mariner's embattled boat?

So give to the monstrous grave
this reluctant prophet, to his tomb
the bridegroom, under the roots
and bars of the rocks, in a mountainous
womb of the sea, bury him deep.

His threnody wails in the wild
wind, while darkness consumes
the sun; naught else avails but death
to render life back to the living.

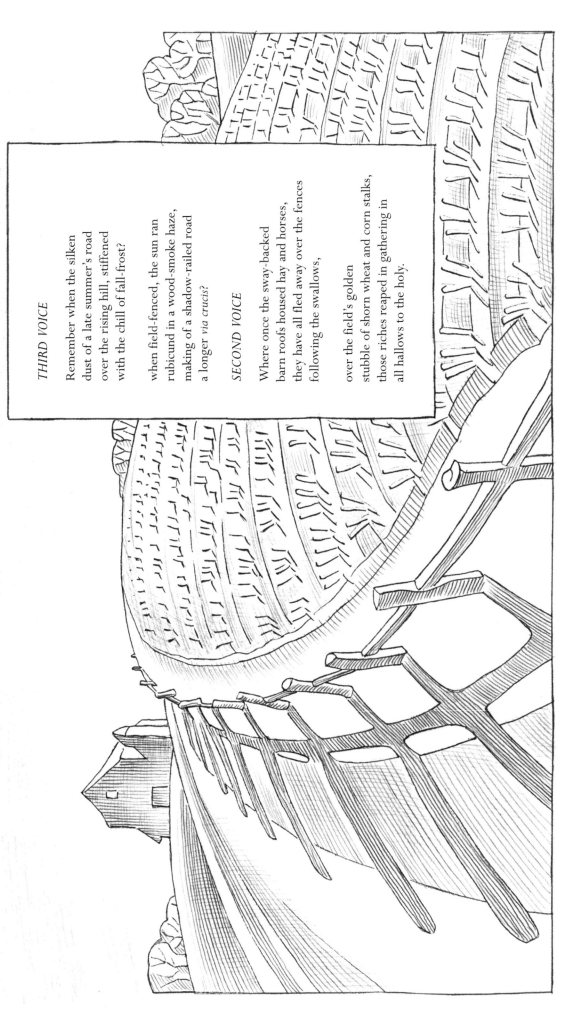

THIRD VOICE

Remember when the silken
dust of a late summer's road
over the rising hill, stiffened
with the chill of fall-frost?

when field-fenced, the sun ran
rubicund in a wood-smoke haze,
making of a shadow-railed road
a longer *via crucis*?

SECOND VOICE

Where once the sway-backed
barn roofs housed hay and horses,
they have all fled away over the fences
following the swallows,

over the field's golden
stubble of shorn wheat and corn stalks,
those riches reaped in gathering in
all hallows to the holy.

SECOND VOICE

Strong arms full of sheaves
of barley and oats, of rice and maize,
millet and wheat, that were loaves
for the hungry, that fed them there,

cornucopias of cucumbers,
melons and leeks, of apples and pears,
vintage in wicker, sanguine and running
with the must of the vine —

all these winged works
have flown to the Father from a workday
world, like songster migrations,
in the harvest of time.

THIRD VOICE

Bales of cotton crops and sheep folds
for clothing the naked, or solacing
the sick with essences medicinal
of barks, roots and herbs,

like a market mirage
of harvesters flying to the fair
over the forest-edged fields and houses
roofed, crying their wares.

119

THE MOURNER

What happened then
must surely seem a dream
of prenatal dawn; I was drifting
calm, over the silver sea
in a luminous mist of morning,

when I saw my infant son;
he was riding his cockleshell,
parting the swell with his
sea-born skiff, on a glimmering
ripple of silver,

with his triton close and held
to his ear, his head inclined in listening,
his smile was a golden lingering, eyes
closed and listening, lost,
O, to the singing sea!

Like a rainbow parhelion
haloed on the circuit it runs,
our small son, my Miriam,
born in the Solstice of winter,
warms to the summering sun.

Your eyes have opened, dearest,
you are awake at last, sorrowful
no longer, your tears of grief have passed;
smile with your laughter longer, love,
and come with me above.

122

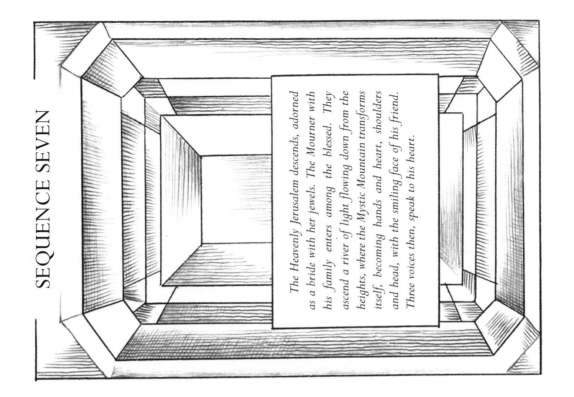

The Heavenly Jerusalem descends, adorned as a bride with her jewels. The Mourner with his family enters among the blessed. They ascend a river of light flowing down from the heights, where the Mystic Mountain transforms itself, becoming hands and heart, shoulders and head, with the smiling face of his friend. Three voices then, speak to his heart.

THE MOURNER

When the envisioned empyreal
descent wrought upon the stellar
fabric, fiery transmutation,
the rent skies widened, where,
crystalline, the city, alight
came down in a bridal
brightness, all diamonded.

And flying, free-fall, these
myriads, dandled in the air
like storm-borne gulls, riding
inland over the river, rose
over the mountain-shadowed,
updraughted lake, and spiraling so
were a very silvering of joy!

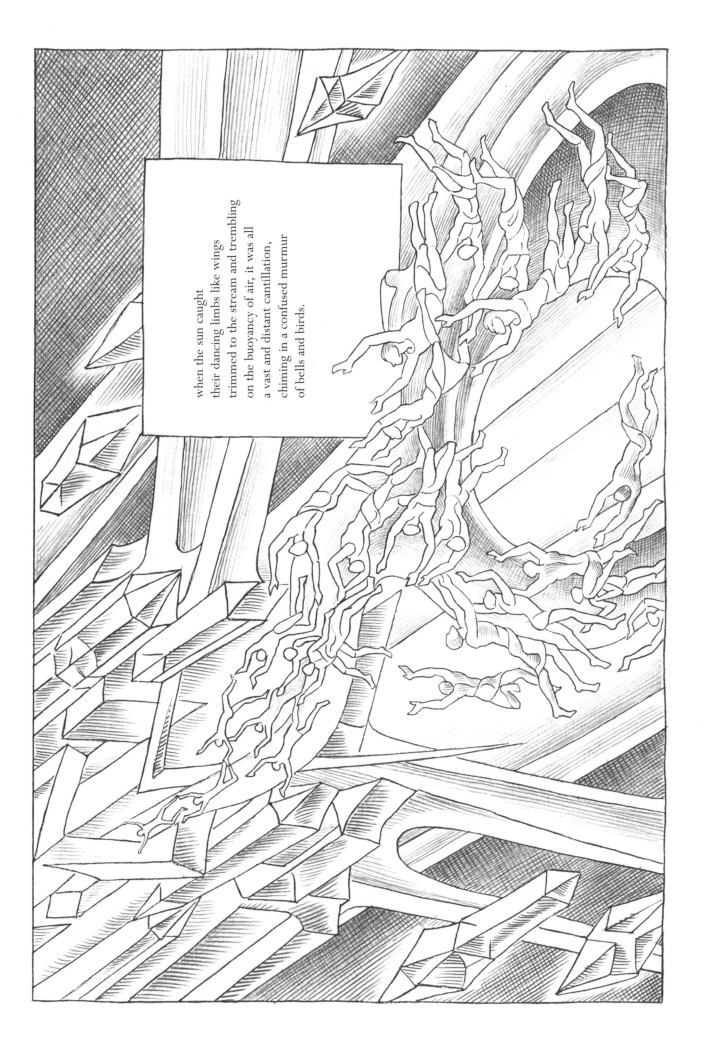

when the sun caught
their dancing limbs like wings
trimmed to the stream and trembling
on the buoyancy of air, it was all
a vast and distant cantillation,
chiming in a confused murmur
of bells and birds.

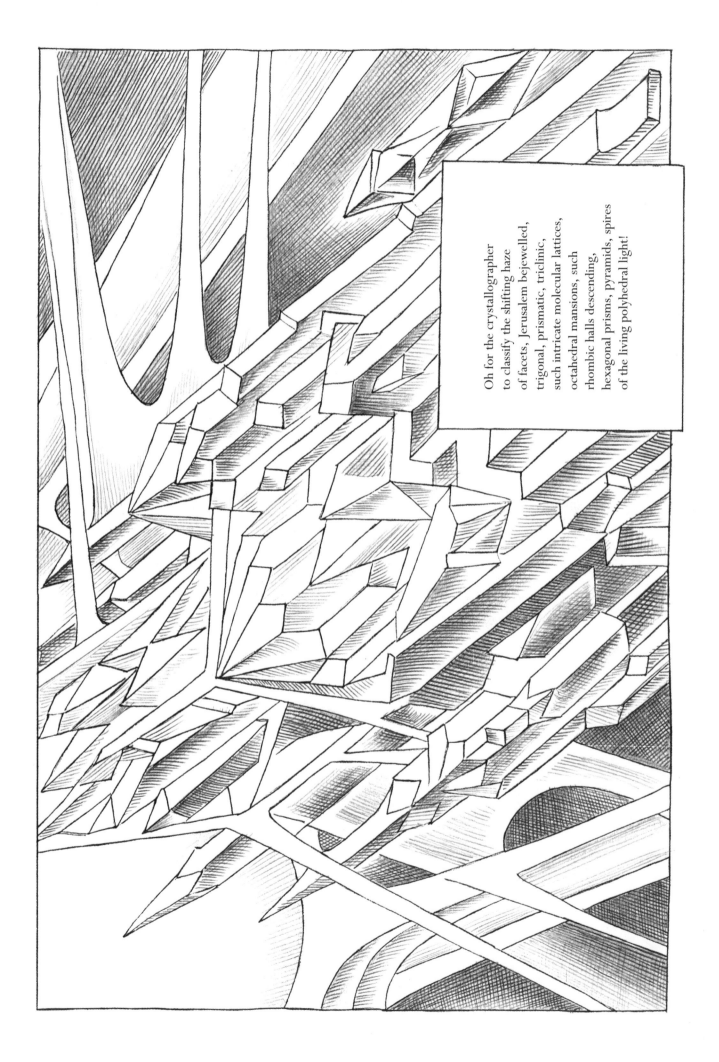

Oh for the crystallographer
to classify the shifting haze
of facets, Jerusalem bejewelled,
trigonal, prismatic, triclinic,
such intricate molecular lattices,
octahedral mansions, such
rhombic halls descending,
hexagonal prisms, pyramids, spires
of the living polyhedral light!

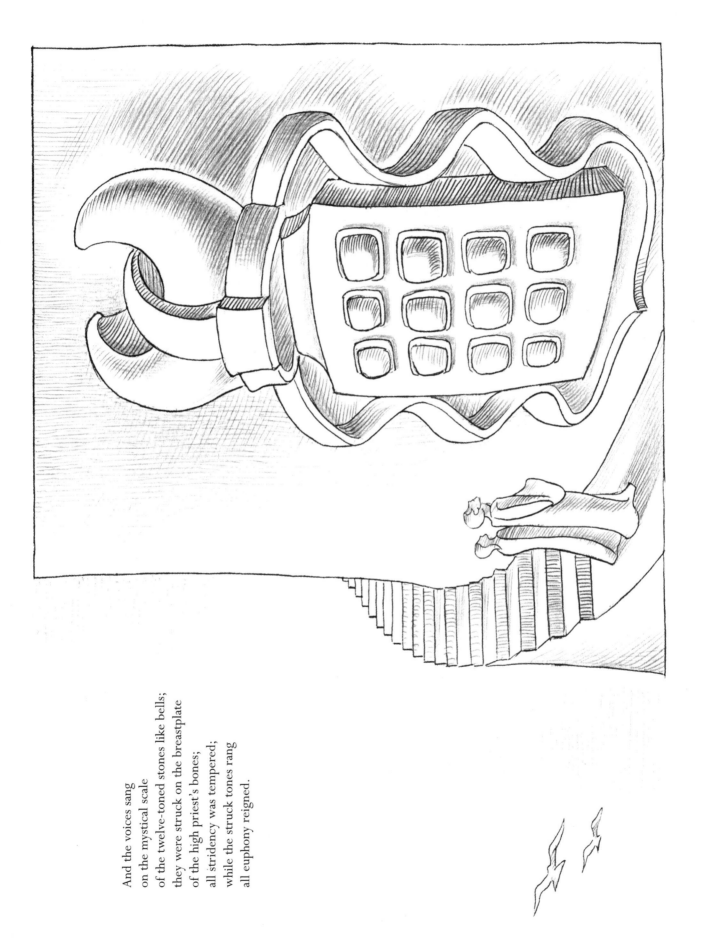

And the voices sang
on the mystical scale
of the twelve-toned stones like bells;
they were struck on the breastplate
of the high priest's bones;
all stridency was tempered;
while the struck tones rang
all euphony reigned.

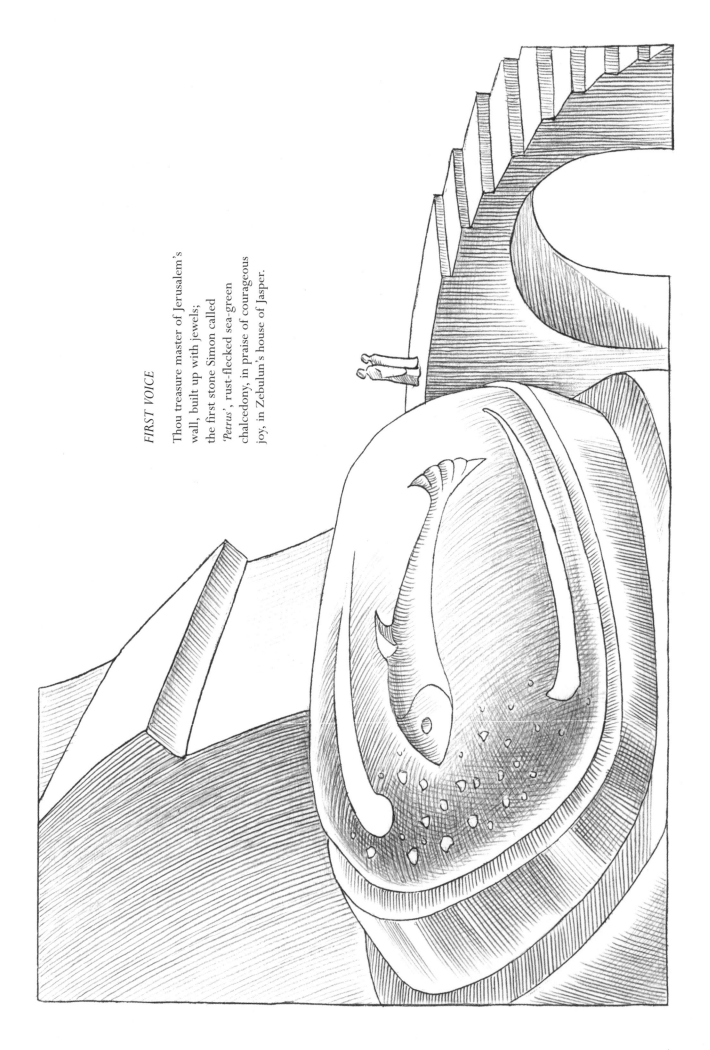

FIRST VOICE

Thou treasure master of Jerusalem's
wall, built up with jewels;
the first stone Simon called
'*Petrus*', rust-flecked sea-green
chalcedony, in praise of courageous
joy, in Zebulun's house of Jasper.

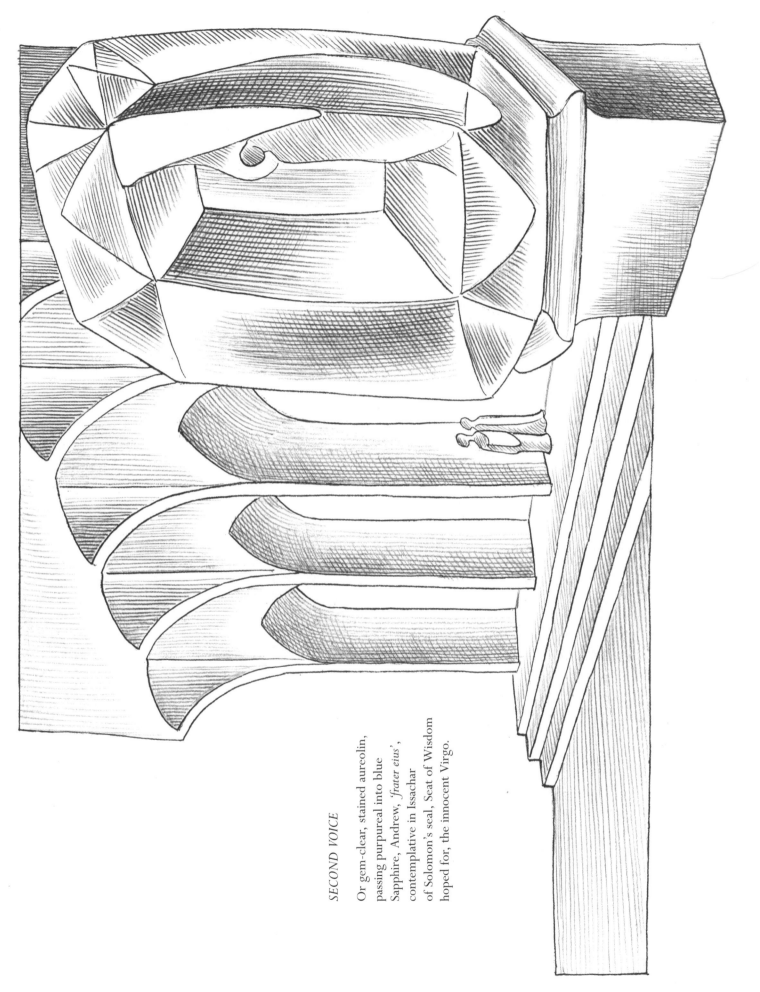

SECOND VOICE

Or gem-clear, stained aureolin,
passing purpureal into blue
Sapphire, Andrew, *'frater eius'*,
contemplative in Issachar
of Solomon's seal, Seat of Wisdom
hoped for, the innocent Virgo.

129

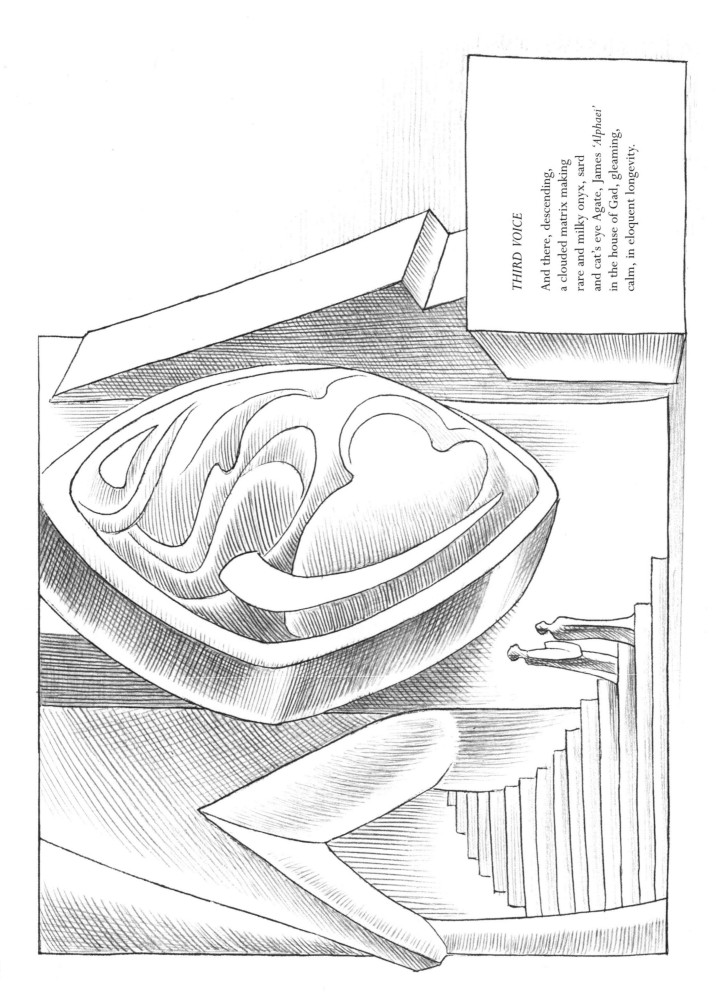

THIRD VOICE

And there, descending,
a clouded matrix making
rare and milky onyx, sard
and cat's eye Agate, James *'Alphaei'*
in the house of Gad, gleaming,
calm, in eloquent longevity.

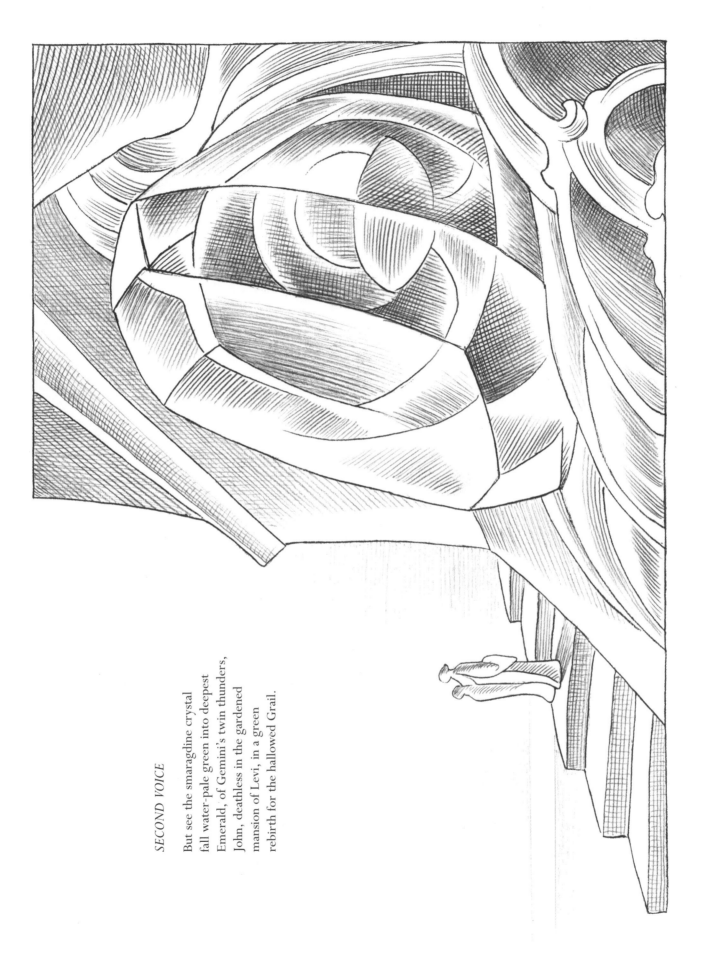

SECOND VOICE

But see the smaragdine crystal
fall water-pale green into deepest
Emerald, of Gemini's twin thunders,
John, deathless in the gardened
mansion of Levi, in a green
rebirth for the hallowed Grail.

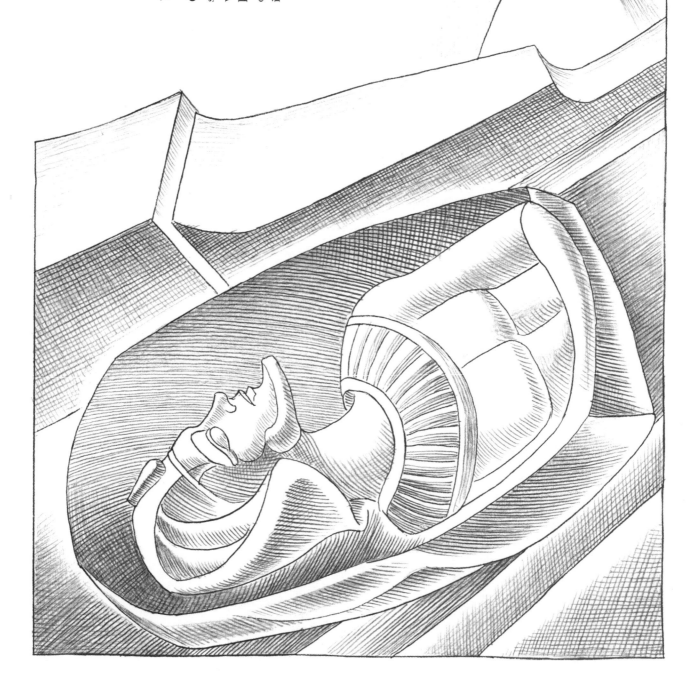

THIRD VOICE

Or the regal descending Sardonyx,
stratified as snow on a bed of fire,
whom Bethsaidan Philip saw and did not
know, Leonine cameo in the household
of Joseph, repelling dreams
in the midnight hour.

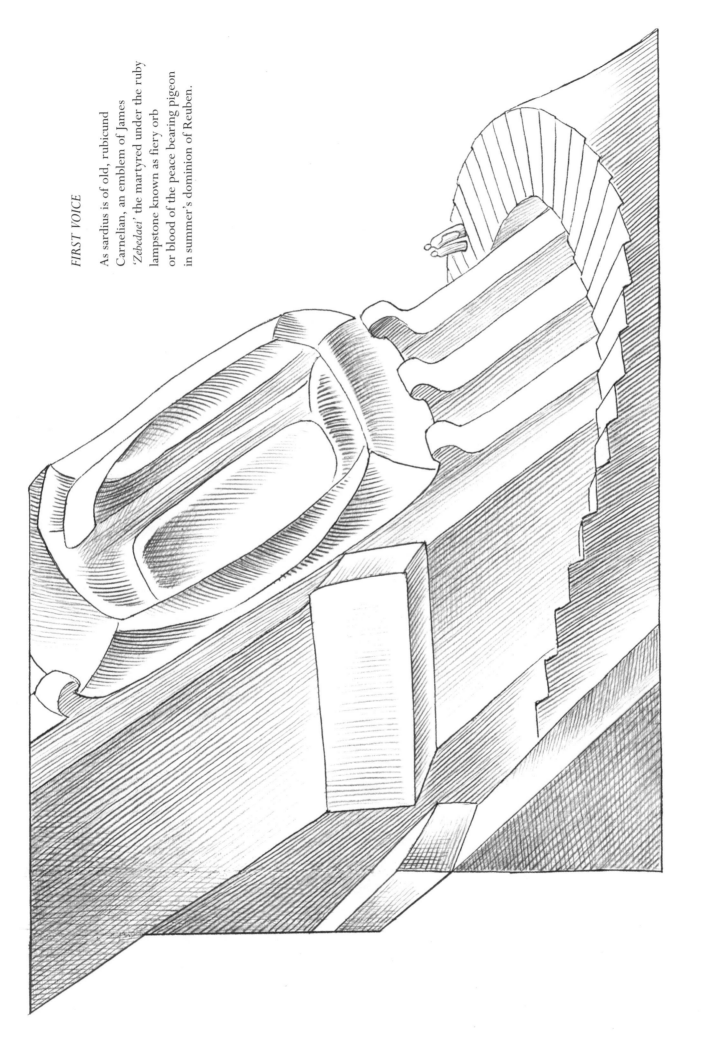

FIRST VOICE

As sardius is of old, rubicund
Carnelian, an emblem of James
'Zebedaei' the martyred under the ruby
lampstone known as fiery orb
or blood of the peace bearing pigeon
in summer's dominion of Reuben.

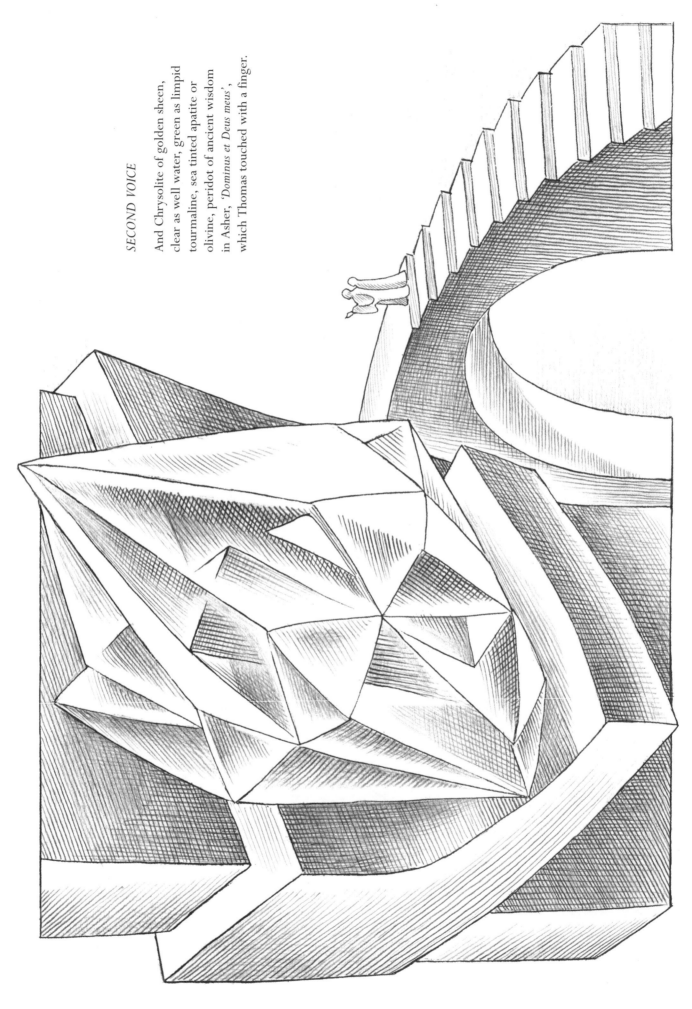

SECOND VOICE

And Chrysolite of golden sheen,
clear as well water, green as limpid
tourmaline, sea tinted apatite or
olivine, peridot of ancient wisdom
in Asher, *'Dominus et Deus meus',*
which Thomas touched with a finger.

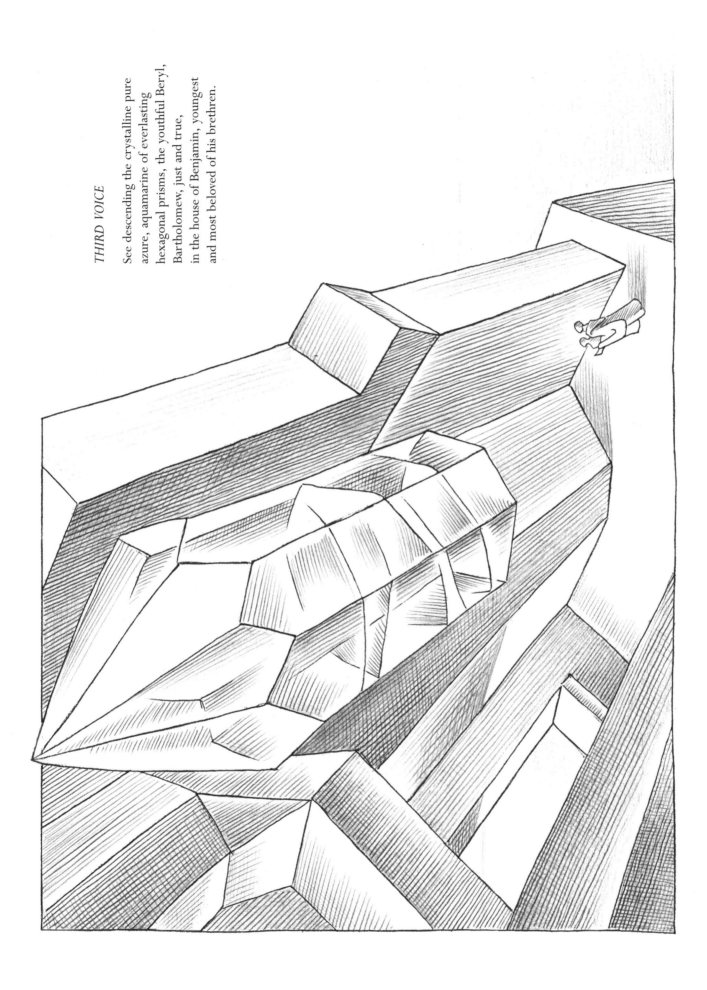

THIRD VOICE

See descending the crystalline pure
azure, aquamarine of everlasting
hexagonal prisms, the youthful Beryl,
Bartholomew, just and true,
in the house of Benjamin, youngest
and most beloved of his brethren.

135

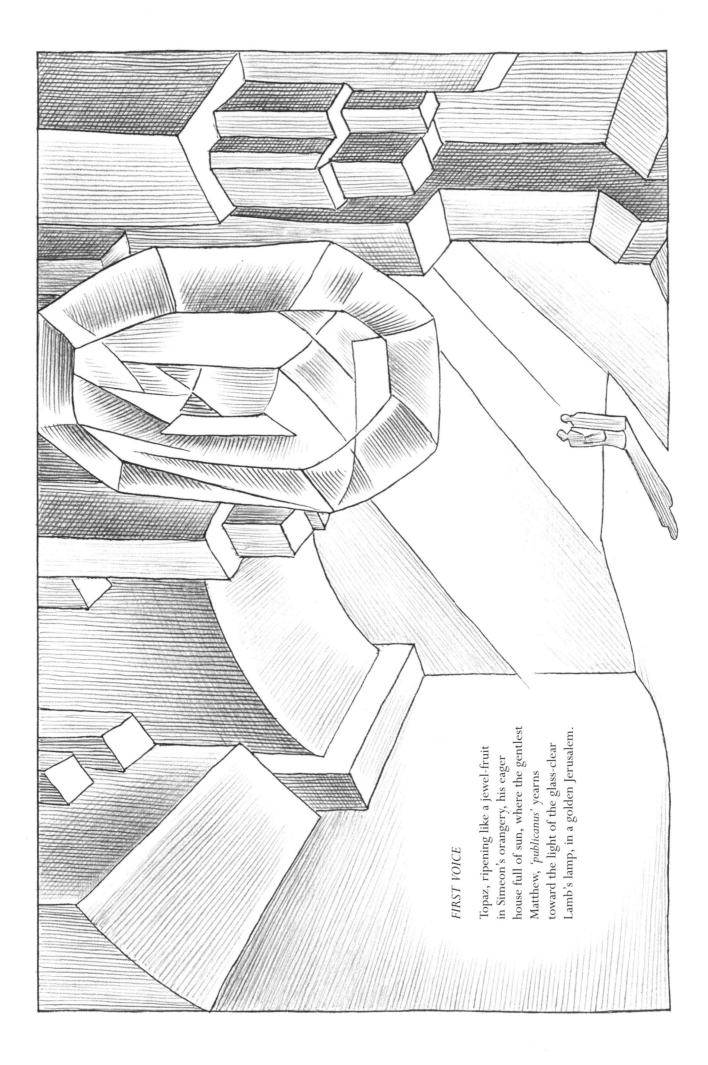

FIRST VOICE

Topaz, ripening like a jewel-fruit
in Simeon's orangery, his eager
house full of sun, where the gentlest
Matthew, 'publicanus', yearns
toward the light of the glass-clear
Lamb's lamp, in a golden Jerusalem.

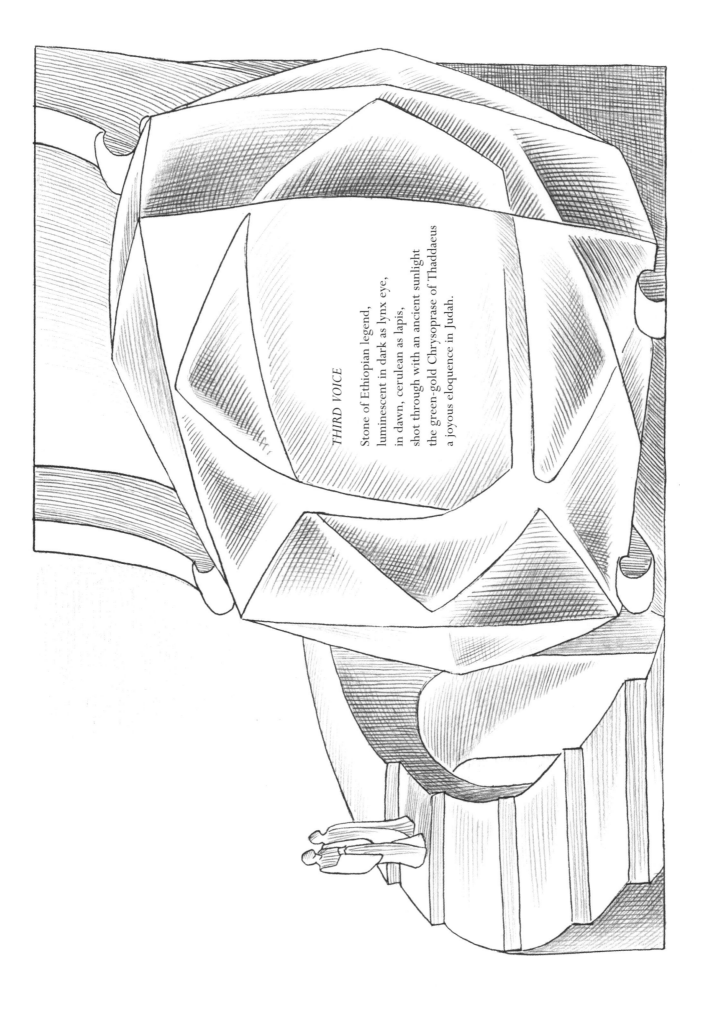

THIRD VOICE

Stone of Ethiopian legend,
luminescent in dark as lynx eye,
in dawn, cerulean as lapis,
shot through with an ancient sunlight
the green-gold Chrysoprase of Thaddaeus
a joyous eloquence in Judah.

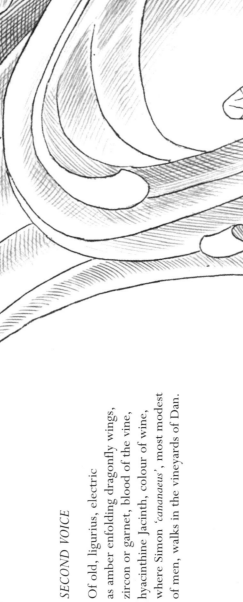

SECOND VOICE

Of old, ligurius, electric
as amber enfolding dragonfly wings,
zircon or garnet, blood of the vine,
hyacinthine Jacinth, colour of wine,
where Simon 'cananaeus', most modest
of men, walks in the vineyards of Dan.

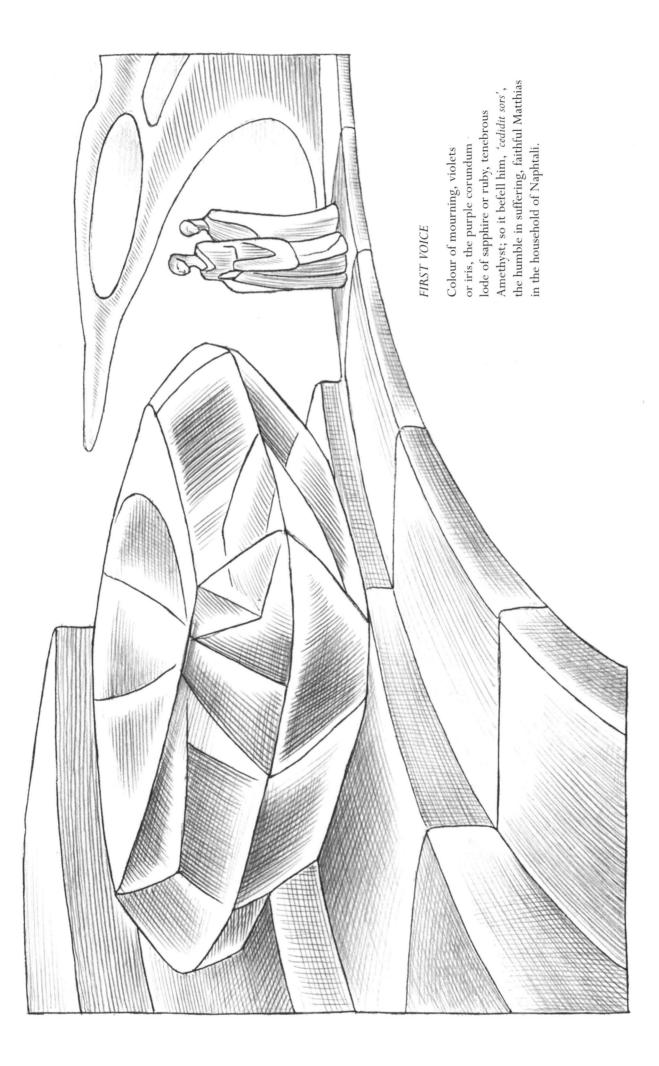

FIRST VOICE

Colour of mourning, violets
or iris, the purple corundum
lode of sapphire or ruby, tenebrous
Amethyst; so it befell him, '*cedidit sors*',
the humble in suffering, faithful Matthias
in the household of Naphtali.

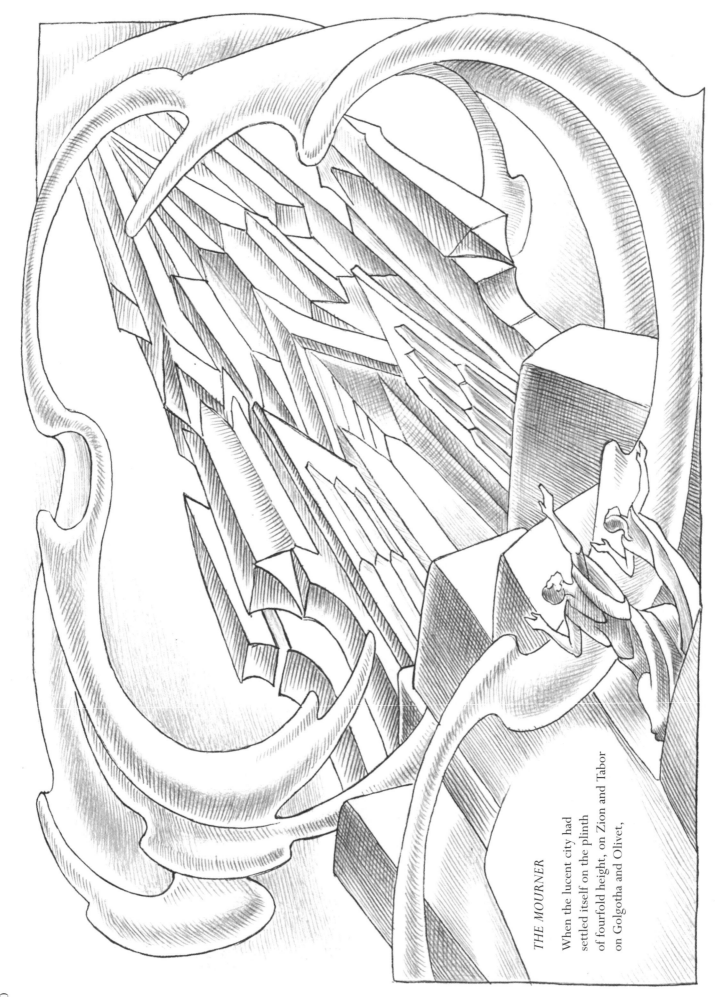

THE MOURNER

When the lucent city had
settled itself on the plinth
of fourfold height, on Zion and Tabor
on Golgotha and Olivet,

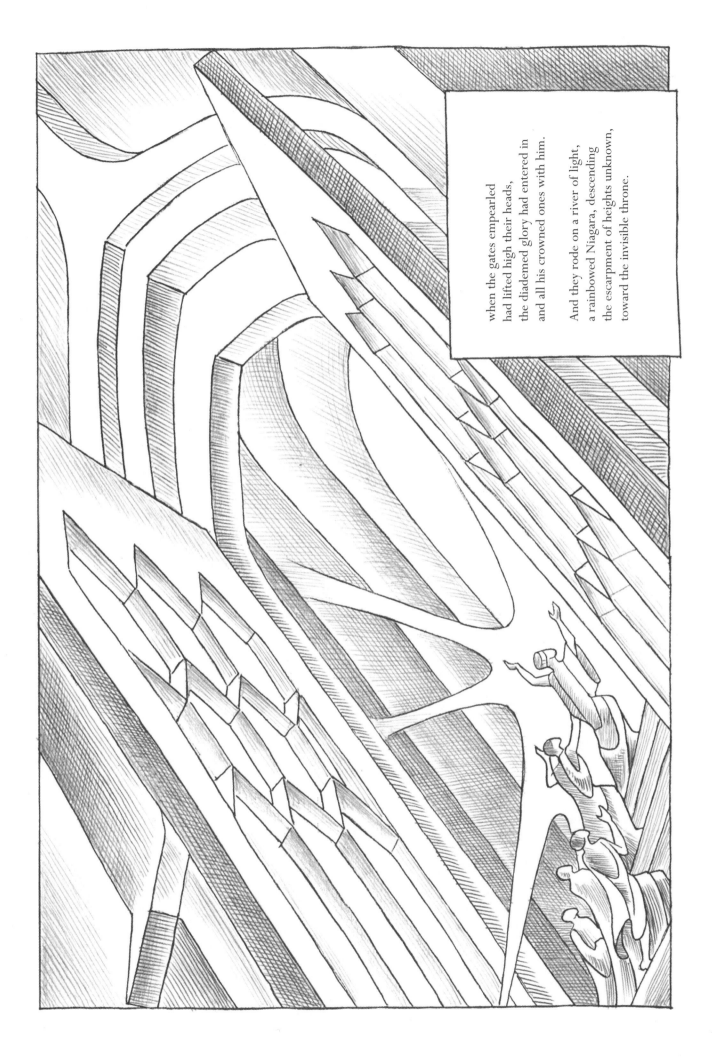

when the gates empearled
had lifted high their heads,
the diademed glory had entered in
and all his crowned ones with him.

And they rode on a river of light,
a rainbowed Niagara, descending
the escarpment of heights unknown,
toward the invisible throne.

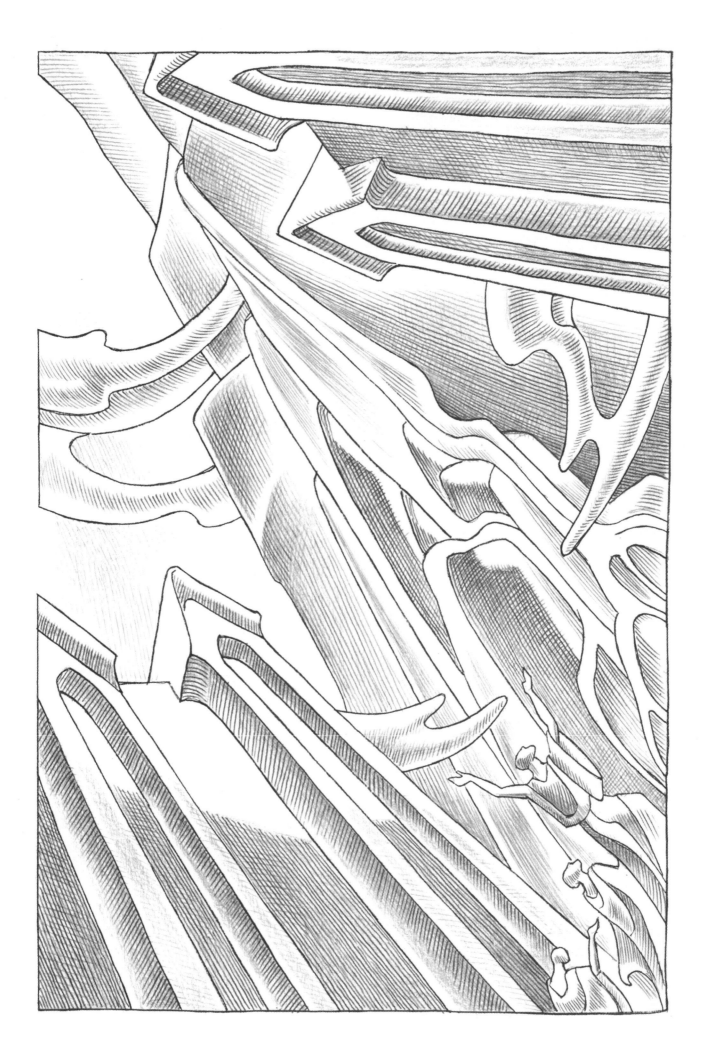

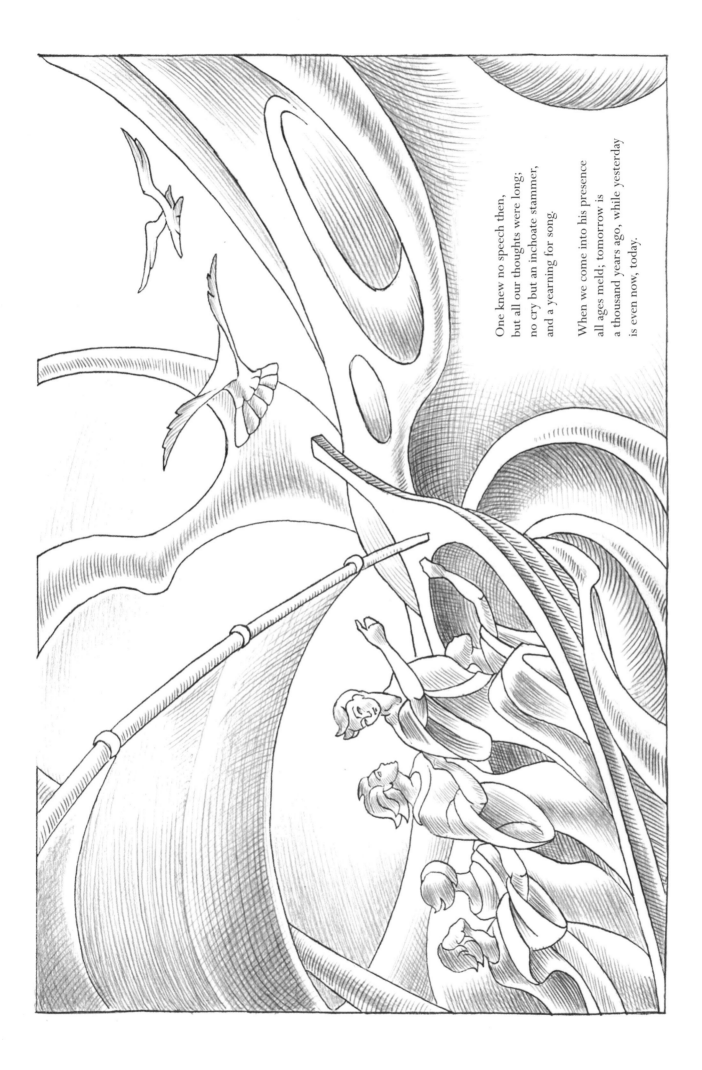

One knew no speech then,
but all our thoughts were long;
no cry but an inchoate stammer,
and a yearning for song.

When we come into his presence
all ages meld; tomorrow is
a thousand years ago, while yesterday
is even now, today.

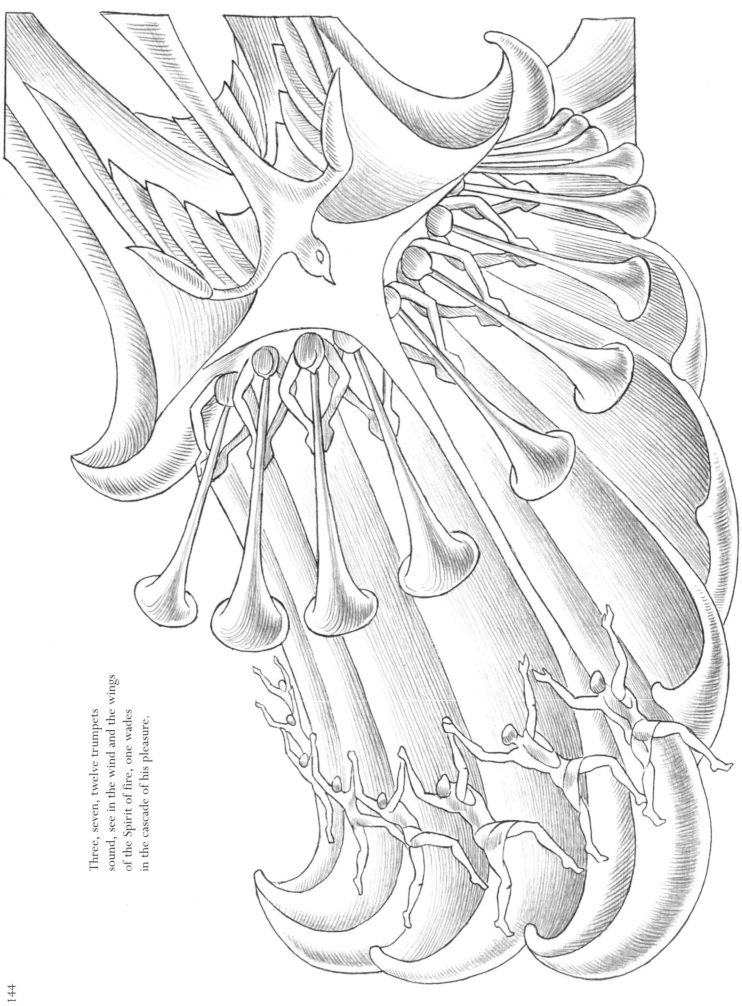

Three, seven, twelve trumpets
sound, see in the wind and the wings
of the Spirit of fire, one wades
in the cascade of his pleasure.

144

As doves, terns, gulls do,
men, birds, eagles fly, they
soar in the rainbows revelling
aloft, and glide without fear.

This mountain moves, once
lifted up, all things unto himself,
that bled such rubies for blood,
shed such diamonds for tears.

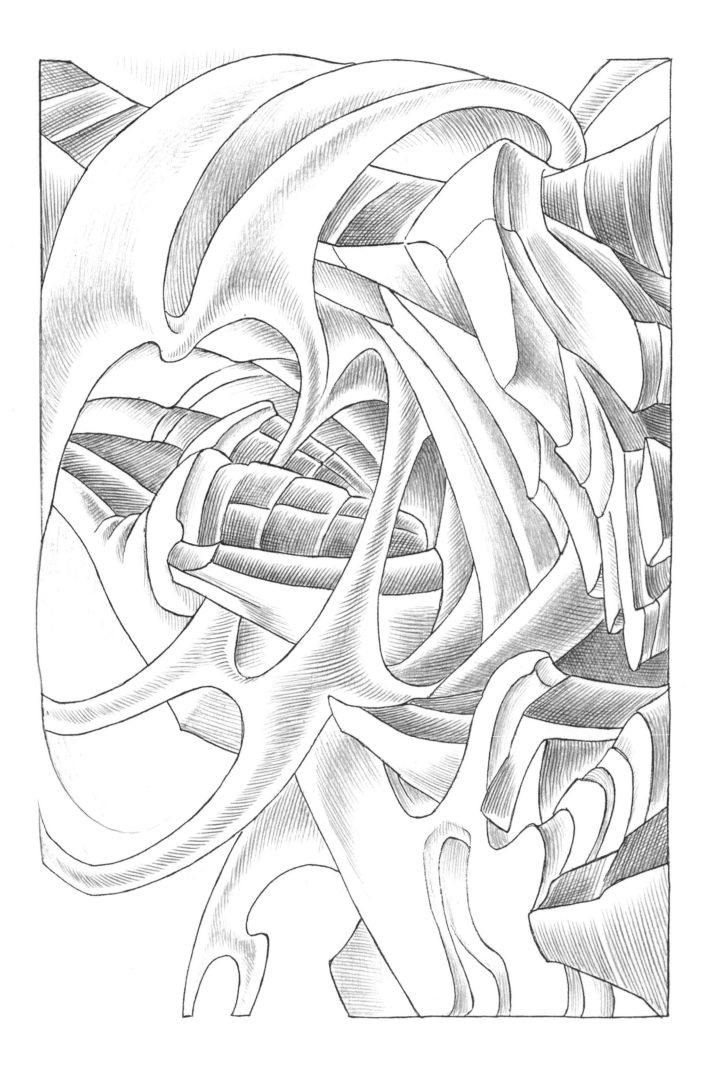

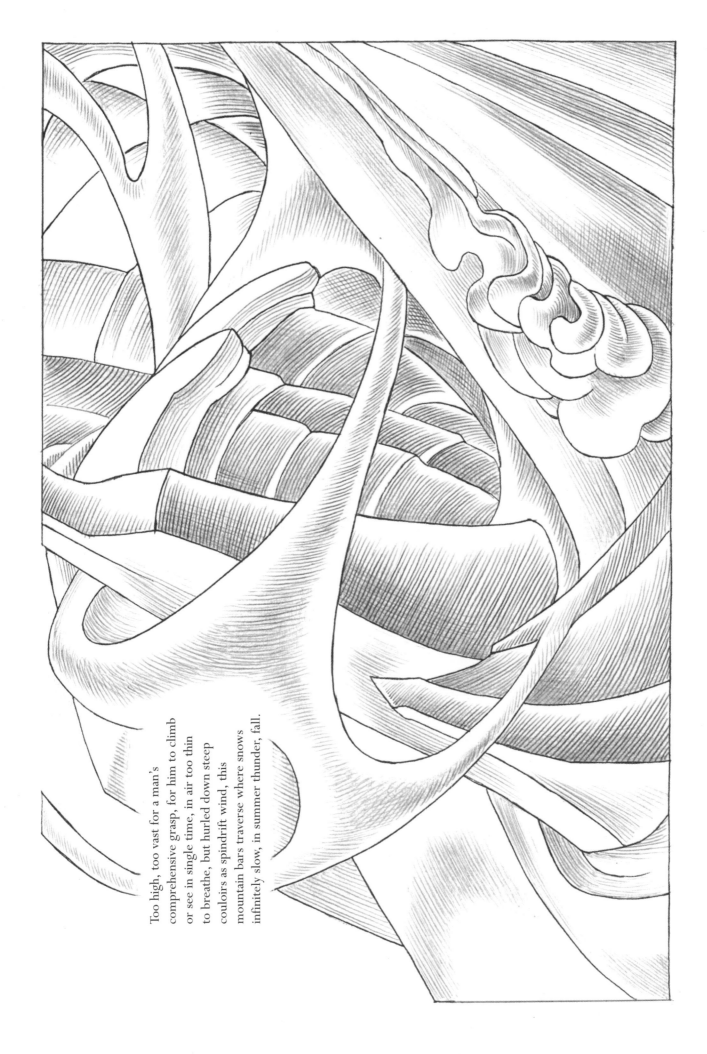

Too high, too vast for a man's comprehensive grasp, for him to climb or see in single time, in air too thin to breathe, but hurled down steep couloirs as spindrift wind, this mountain bars traverse where snows infinitely slow, in summer thunder, fall.

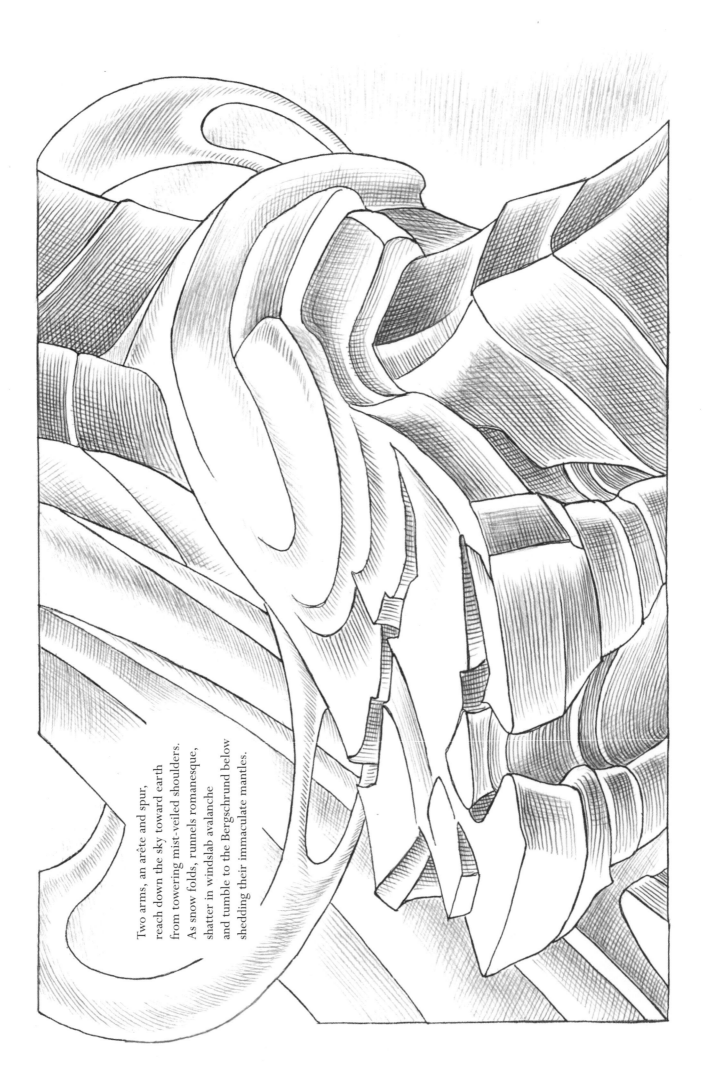

Two arms, an arête and spur,
reach down the sky toward earth
from towering mist-veiled shoulders.
As snow folds, runnels romanesque,
shatter in windslab avalanche
and tumble to the Bergschrund below
shedding their immaculate mantles.

There emerge, with a ricochet of answering echoes, rock-hewn, under vestments of ice, the alabastrine hands wrought in clefts, their veins of marble shed from a motherlode of gems, embers of mountain magma.

149

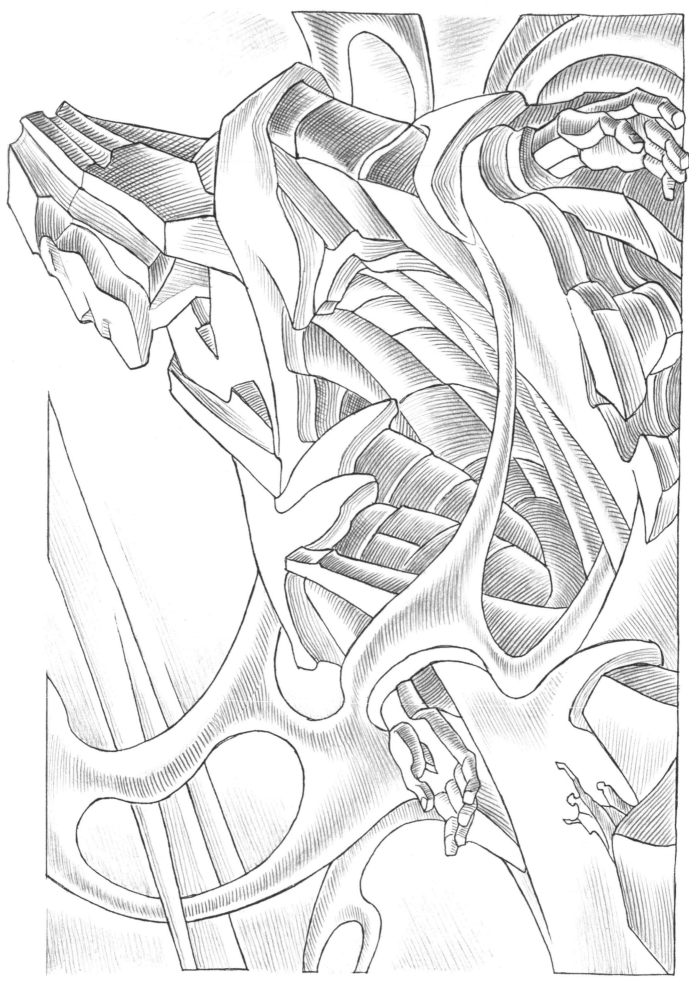

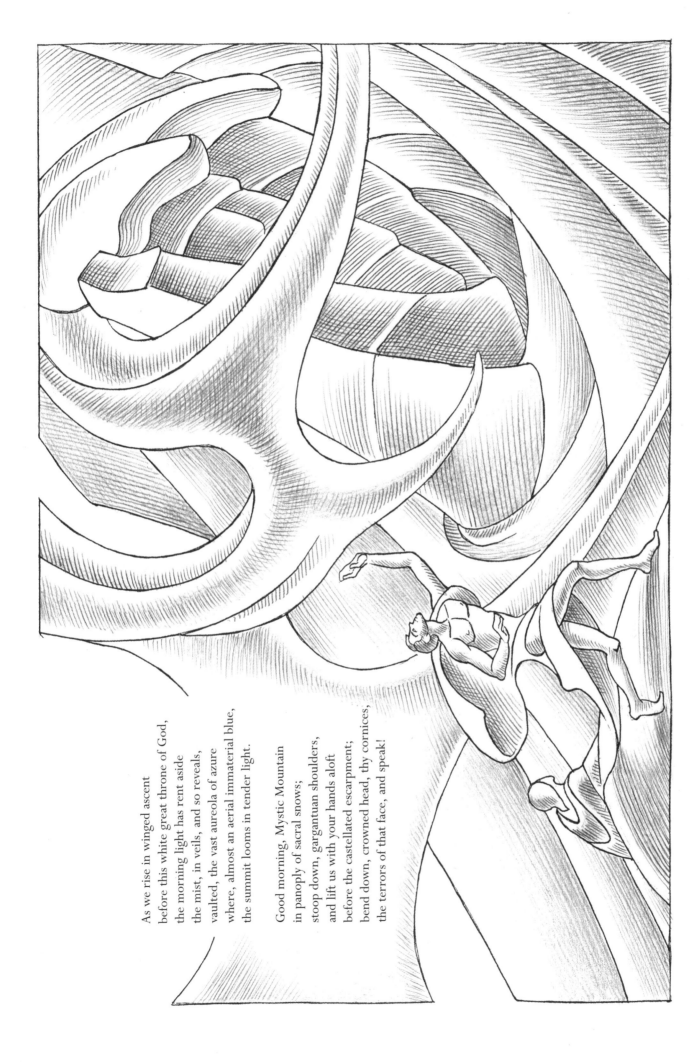

As we rise in winged ascent
before this white great throne of God,
the morning light has rent aside
the mist, in veils, and so reveals,
vaulted, the vast aureola of azure
where, almost an aerial immaterial blue,
the summit looms in tender light.

Good morning, Mystic Mountain
in panoply of sacral snows;
stoop down, gargantuan shoulders,
and lift us with your hands aloft
before the castellated escarpment;
bend down, crowned head, thy cornices,
the terrors of that face, and speak!

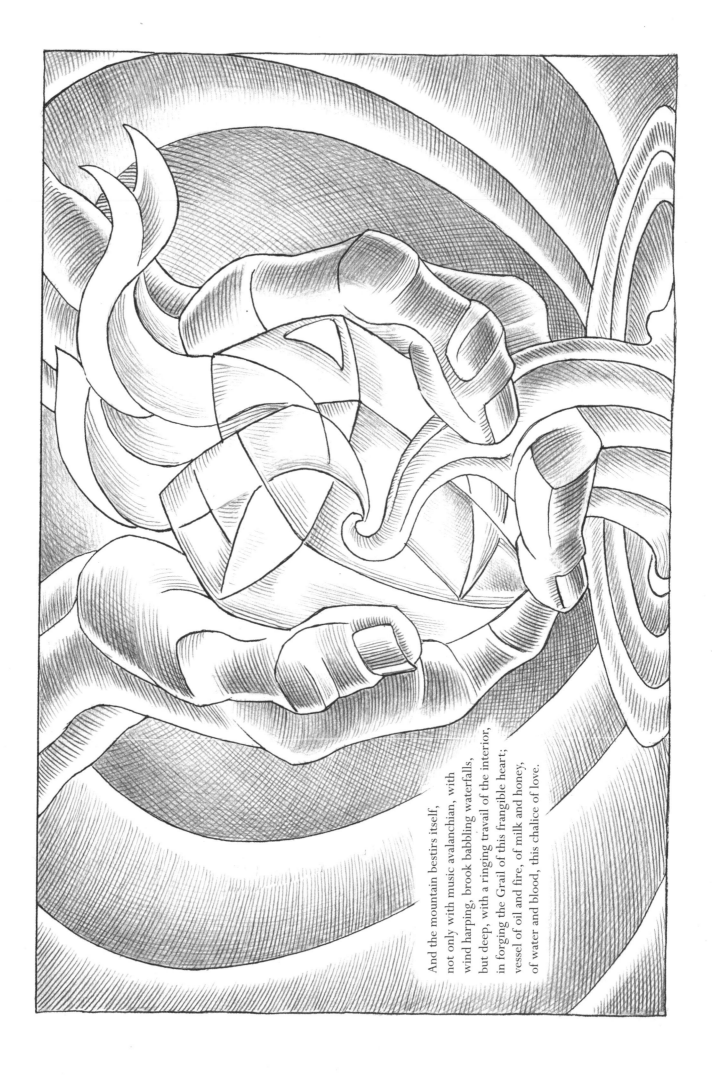

And the mountain bestirs itself,
not only with music avalanchian, with
wind harping, brook babbling waterfalls,
but deep, with a ringing travail of the interior,
in forging the Grail of this frangible heart;
vessel of oil and fire, of milk and honey,
of water and blood, this chalice of love.

I begin to see, begin to understand
this most mysterious transformation
of mountain into man; it is he, my friend,
the once rejected, yet laid in Zion now,
a cornerstone and temple keystone
once destroyed, yet raised anew —
no, I am not crazed — it is true!

The Mountain gathers us in arms
of linen-like snow and silken light;
his voice is bounding like alpenhorns
echoing upon the heights; in smiling
alabaster his face bends down, welcoming;
his crown is a wedding of lights; Rabboni
Master, speak, I know it is Thee I see —

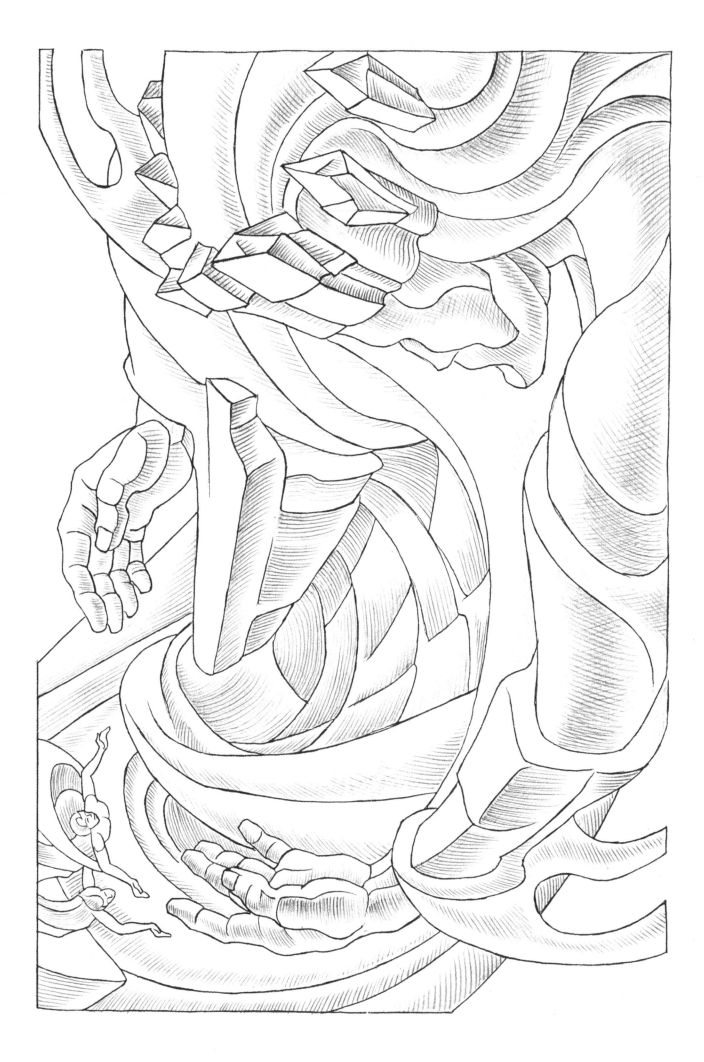

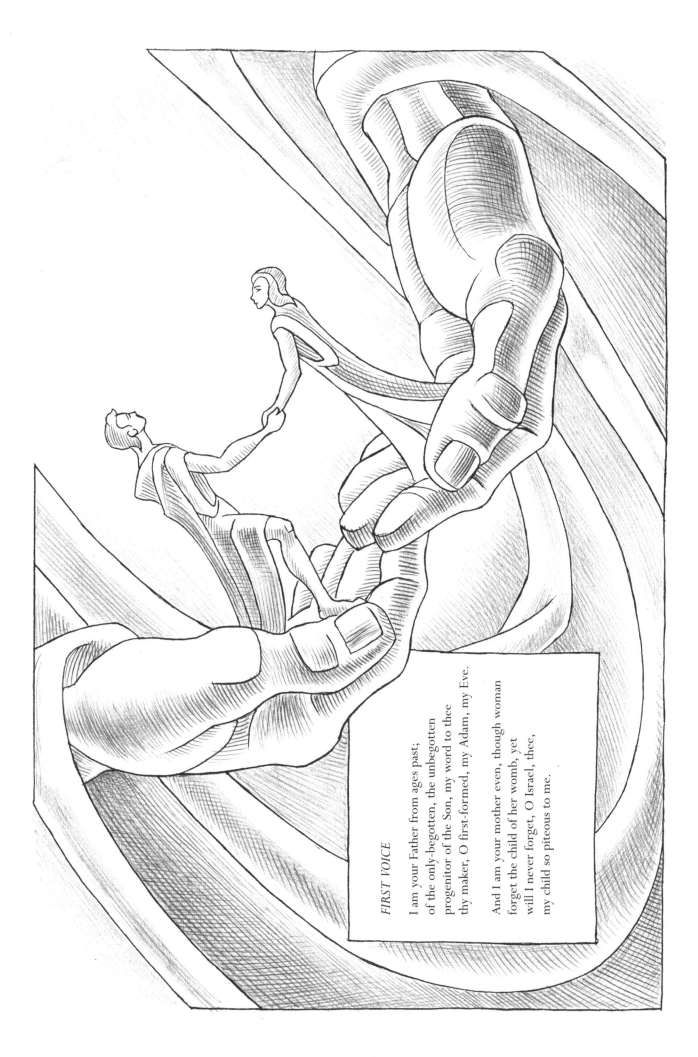

FIRST VOICE

I am your Father from ages past;
of the only-begotten, the unbegotten
progenitor of the Son, my word to thee
thy maker, O first-formed, my Adam, my Eve.

And I am your mother even, though woman
forget the child of her womb, yet
will I never forget, O Israel, thee,
my child so piteous to me.

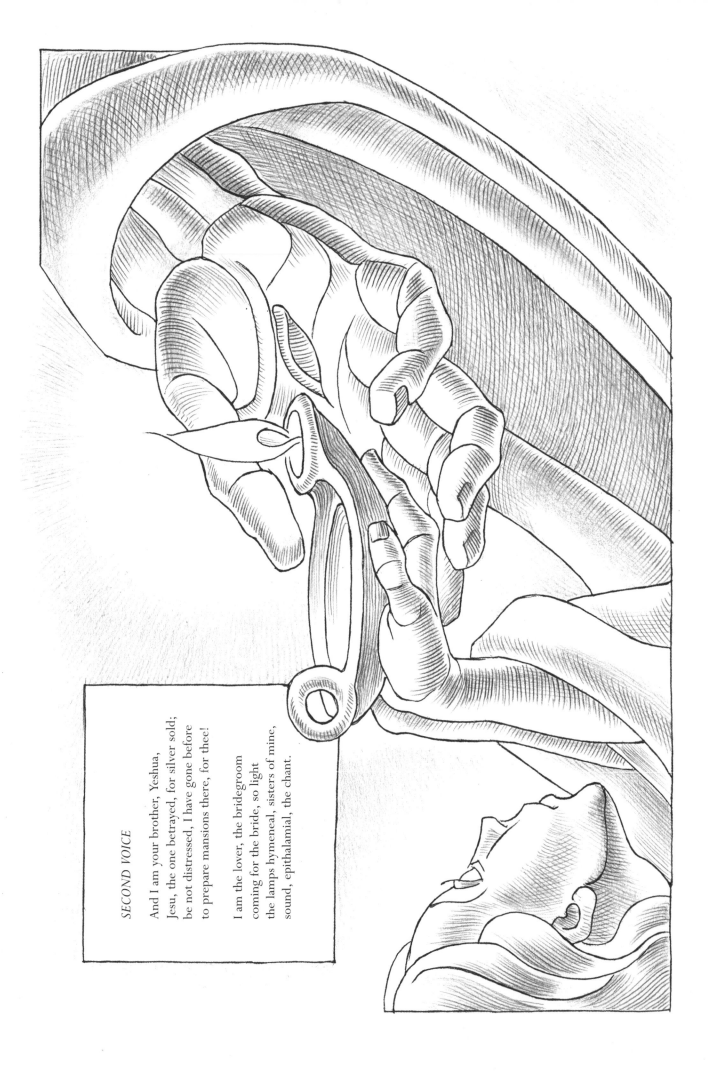

SECOND VOICE

And I am your brother, Yeshua,
Jesu, the one betrayed, for silver sold;
be not distressed, I have gone before
to prepare mansions there, for thee!

I am the lover, the bridegroom
coming for the bride, so light
the lamps hymeneal, sisters of mine,
sound, epithalamial, the chant.

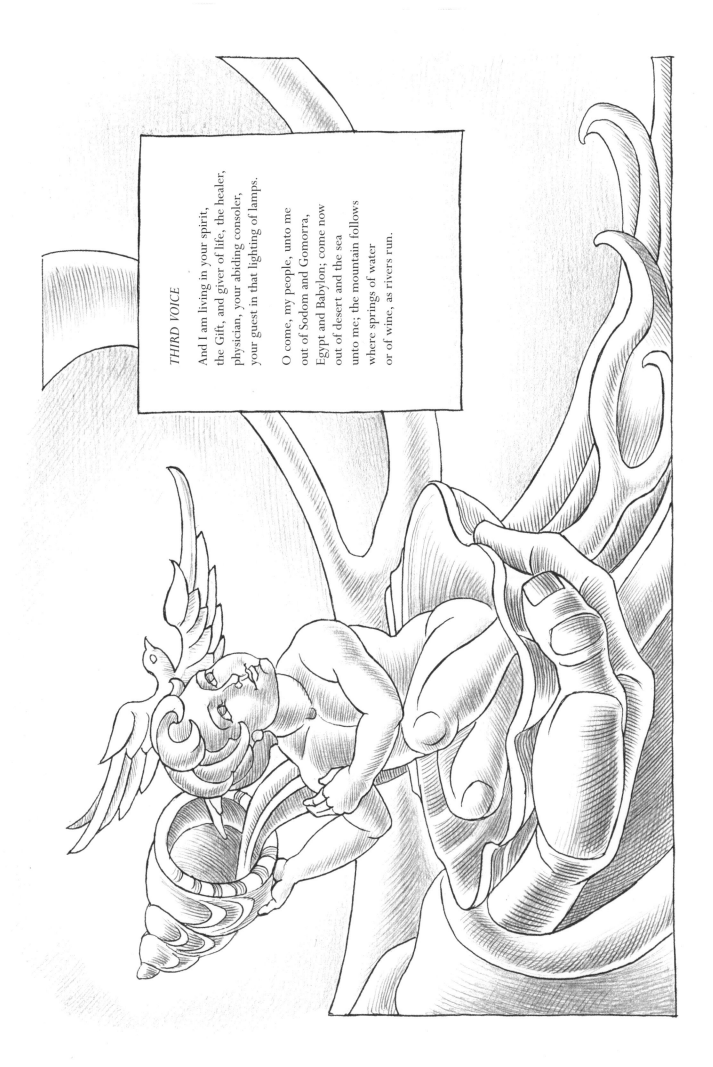

THIRD VOICE

And I am living in your spirit,
the Gift, and giver of life, the healer,
physician, your abiding consoler,
your guest in that lighting of lamps.

O come, my people, unto me
out of Sodom and Gomorra,
Egypt and Babylon; come now
out of desert and the sea
unto me; the mountain follows
where springs of water
or of wine, as rivers run.

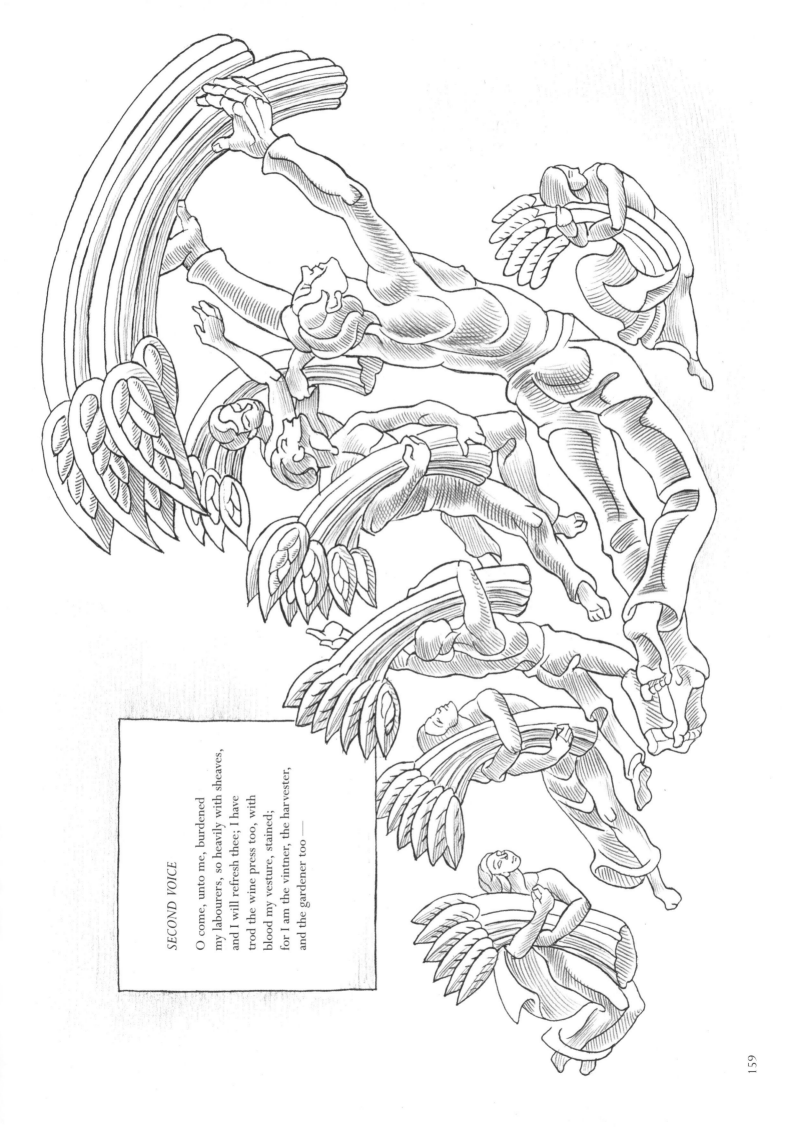

SECOND VOICE

O come, unto me, burdened
my labourers, so heavily with sheaves,
and I will refresh thee; I have
trod the wine press too, with
blood my vesture, stained;
for I am the vintner, the harvester,
and the gardener too —

I am the Sower and the seed;
so come as I call thee
my sister, and brother,
and mother, unto me.

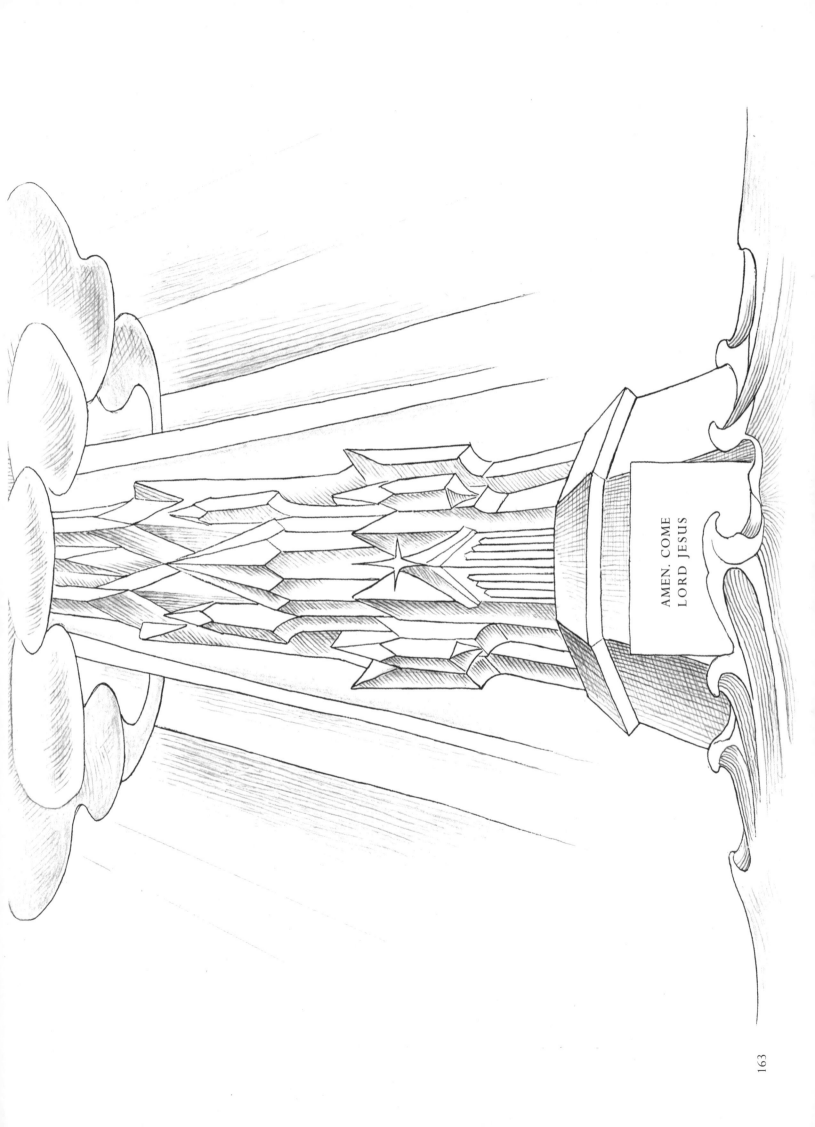

AFTERWORD

The genesis of *The Mystic Mountain* goes back to October 1962, some twenty-nine years ago. It began as a collaboration with Anthony Collins, a young film maker who saw possibilities in a stained glass window I had designed for the crypt of the Abbey's bell tower.

The imagery of this window was derived from St Paul's First Epistle to the Corinthians, chapter fifteen, where he speaks of the manner of the resurrection. In this passage we find the sower, and the seed which must die to bring forth fruit; the earthly but differing bodies of men, birds and fish; the heavenly bodies of sun, moon and stars which differ from each other in glory, also how the earthly Adam must die to put on the heavenly man, Christ; and finally the trumpet of the resurrection, when we shall be changed — what is mortal becoming immortal. 'O death, where is thy victory? O death, where is thy sting?'

Five Latin stanzas were written embodying these Pauline thoughts, and were subsequently set for choral voices by Canadian composer Elliot Weisgarber. An English version of the spoken voice was also written. When Collins moved to Montreal in 1964, we had to abandon the use of the window. The graphics, totally redesigned, were to be painted and shot on multiple levels. At the same time, the Prologue was partly written, clarifying the storyline of a man mourning his dead wife and son. I began making sketches — the house in the empty street, the funeral cortege, the open grave. The imagery was substantially that of the present work. The first five sequences correspond to the Latin stanzas, while the last two accommodate the alleluias added by the composer. Unfortunately, by this time, the film had grown too complex for our means, and in 1967 its production had to be abandoned.

All the technical notes and drawings went into my files to be occasionally dreamed about over the next sixteen years. Then, in 1984, I began to think about the possibility of an illustrated book of poetry based on the film. The publisher Carl Siegler was interested enough to read my materials and to advise me. He suggested connecting the short stanzas with more poetry. I began writing at once, and it was not long before I realized that what I was writing was a poetic scenario. The manuscript was completed on Good Friday, 1986.

A word about the voices. Originally there was only one voice for the Friend in the Prologue. The length of the poem, however, required more perspectives, more variation. So the one voice became three. As the writing progressed, the voices became more and more mysterious. Each developed its distinct personality. I knew by the end who the Friend was, and who the voices were. There is one other voice, the Priest. He is doubled by the second voice, for appropriate theological reasons.

D.M.
Westminster Abbey
Mission, B.C.
June 1991

NOTES

The sources of the poem are many. There are, of course, those great massifs of the epic mode — Homer, Dante, Milton. One does not easily escape their shadows. But more immediately, stemming from the monastic celebration of the Liturgy and the psalmody of the Hours, there are allusions, paraphrases and a few quotations from the Old and New Testaments of the Bible. Central to the whole symbolism, Paul's fifteenth chapter of First Corinthians, has already been mentioned.

Leviathan in the Second Sequence was sighted in the third and fortieth chapters of the Book of Job, while Jonah, the reluctant prophet, who appears in the Third Sequence, was pressed into service from the first two chapters of his book. This is paralleled by an allusion to Matthew, chapter twelve, about the Son of Man's three days and nights in the heart of the earth (see pages 33 to 35, and 43, 44).

In the Fourth Sequence the tidal wave had its beginnings in chapter twenty-one of St Luke, while the rattling of the bones in the Fifth Sequence obviously echoes the thirty-seventh chapter of Ezekiel. St John chapter five contributes the pool of Bethesda as a site for the beginning of a new life (see pages 67, 84 following, and 101, 102).

In Sequence Six, I borrowed St Matthew's dragnet from chapter thirteen, and in the Seventh and final Sequence, St John's great white throne, his jewels, his heavenly Jerusalem — how shall I ever repay my indebtedness? I was consoled to discover that John himself had borrowed his jewels from Exodus, chapter twenty-eight (see pages 106, 124, 129 following, and 151).

Then the Transfiguration in Matthew seventeen, a theophany of three: Christ in glory, the voice of the Father, and the bright cloud of the Holy Spirit. The Mountain? I have no intention of listing the innumerable mountains in the Old and New Testaments. Paul's 'Rock of Christ', First Corinthians, chapter ten, is important, as is the final intimacy of 'brother and sister and mother' from St Matthew, chapter twelve. There are others, but the reader will have to ferret them out (see pages 140, 147 following, and 151 to 153).

The double astrological symbolism in the Third Sequence requires some explanation. It gave me a somewhat perverse pleasure to filch from Carl Sagan's book, *Cosmos* (he being an atheist), the idea he mentions of a German monk, Julius Schiller, who attempted in 1627 to supplant the pagan mythology of the skies with a Christian hagiography. I record this to acknowledge my indebtedness.

As a result, Eridanus, Phaethon's fatal river, becomes the river of life, and the navigator's Piscis, the Star of the Sea. The disguised Capricorn, as Pan, is banished by Aquarius, the water bearer, who is of course, the Baptist, while the sun's Ecliptic in that constellation makes the Baptist himself defer to the one who is the true Sun of Justice. Then again, Cetus, the storm bringer, becomes the biblical whale swallowing down the reluctant prophet, who is, in turn, only the foreshade of Christ harrowing old Sheol of its dead. I trust some New Age astrologer will be taken in my net, for it's not the stars that save, but the Maker of the stars (see pages 41 to 44).

At this point, the Sequence modulates from mythology to astrophysics, where God's hand shows itself even more. It's my belief that any astronomer must ultimately ask how the vast, rationally coherent and discoverable process could have arisen without a supreme intelligence to order it. I'm thinking of the birth, death, and rebirth of a single star. The gravitational contraction of the hydrogenous cloud till nuclear fusion into helium ignites that star for billions of years must surely manifest a true creation of cosmos out of chaos. When the fuel of a star is depleted and the helium core itself ignites in the continuing crush, the star becomes a Phoenix arisen from its own ashes. Its burning continues till the core is pure iron, and all the elements save the heaviest, are layered in its fiery envelope.

When that iron core collapses in the catastrophic explosion of a Super Nova, it falls into a black hole from which even light cannot escape, leaving behind a dower of silver and gold — the rings on your fingers, and the fillings in your teeth! I see the hand of God in this gigantic crucible, forging the elements of a new heaven and a new earth (see pages 48 to 51).

Astronomical data was derived from *The Stars In Their Courses*, Sir James Jeans (Macmillan Co., 1931); Carl Sagan's *Cosmos* (Random House, New York, 1980); and the *National Geographic Picture Atlas of Our Universe*, by Roy A. Gallant, 1980.

In writing the last two Sequences I had a problem. What is it like moving from time into Eternity? How could I express the inexpressible? 'The instant ages meld;' was a stammering attempt; time no longer drags like a weight — no waiting for tomorrow — no pining for yesterday. I rifled the *Summa Theologiae* of St Thomas Aquinas, Prima Pars, regarding time and eternity in six articles; one, very important, on aeviternity — the half-way state. And then, in Tertia Pars, the questions dealing with the last things, and the condition of those resurrected — what is it like? The cause and manner of rising — from whose dust after the fire? Whose identity — am I myself? Then the bodily qualities — the inability to suffer; the subtle appearance at will, or passing through the locked doors; the rapid agility to move like thought, and the shining clarity. How shall we sing of it? How articulate the new heaven and the new earth; the vision of God's being, the happiness, the mansions, the gifts, the aureoles? What Aquinas thought, Dante sums up in a Rose, and I myself? — in a Mountain (see pages 145 following).

The jewels in the Seventh Sequence we have already mentioned, but not the complexities of their identification. The twelve stones listed in Exodus, 28:15–21, are variously assigned to the twelve tribes of Israel, whose names were engraved upon them. Our sources are the Greek Septuagint, 270 B.C., the historian Josephus, writing in Greek, 90 A.D., St Jerome's Latin Vulgate, 400 A.D., and the English versions, the Douay, 1609 A.D., the Authorised Version 1611 A.D. with its revision in 1884 A.D. Besides these there are other Talmudic and Occult sources which are even more complex. Just as John's apocalyptic enumeration of the gems modifies the Mosaic one in Exodus, so in each of these traditions the gems themselves undergo bewildering transformations. In naming the jewels for the Apostles, I have assumed St John would have followed Matthew's enumeration of the twelve in assigning their order. But even here, folkloric tradition has overcome in several instances the expected order. Judas Iscariot has been replaced as in the Acts of the Apostles, by the elected Matthias. In the twelve lapidary stanzas I have not hesitated to use both the ancient and modern names, since the words themselves are gems with which to adorn the bride (see pages 126 to 139). Some mythological lore was derived from the *Dictionary of Mythology, Folklore and Symbols* by Gertrude Jobes (The Scarecrow Press, Inc., New York, 1962).

	Jewels:	Tribes of Israel:	Twelve Apostles:
1	Jasper	Zebulun	Peter (Simon)
2	Sapphire	Issachar	Andrew (his brother)
3	Agate	Gad	James (son of Alphaeus)
4	Emerald	Levi	John
5	Sardonyx	Joseph	Philip (of Bethsaida)
6	Carnelian	Reuben	James (son of Zebedee)
7	Chrysolite	Asher	Thomas (my Lord & my God)

8	Beryl	Benjamin	Bartholomew
9	Topaz	Simeon	Matthew (tax collector)
10	Chrysoprase	Judah	Thaddaeus
11	Jacinth	Dan	Simon (the Cananaean)
12	Amethyst	Naphtali	Matthias (elected)

Ichthys. Greek word for fish. Because the letters of the word form the notarikon of the Greek phrase Iesous CHristos THeou Uios Soter (Jesus Christ, Son of God, Saviour), the fish was used as a symbol by the early Christians (see page 32).

'Myth and mysterium' — *Mysterium fidei*, the ancient invitation of the people in the Eucharistic prayer to proclaim the 'mystery of faith'. The Friend invites assent to the hidden manna in the allegory (see page 44).

Jonathan crucified. The Mourner fails to recognise the image of the sacrificial Christ in the dolphin and Ichthys. Jonathan transfixed to the anchor of hope reveals his baptism into the Lord's mystery of death and resurrection (see page 68).

Tenebrae. From the Latin for shadows, or darkness. Pre-Vatican II liturgy of Matins and Lauds, sung on the evening before Wednesday, Thursday, and Friday of Holy Week. Twelve candles were extinguished one by one during the psalmody to symbolise the Apostles' abandonment of Christ. A wooden clapper, rattled by the acolyte, represented the death of the Lord and the earthquake (see page 76).

Orante. A praying figure, often portrayed in the catacombs with hands raised. In death itself, the spirit prays for life (see page 102).

'Amen. Come Lord Jesus'. From Revelation 22:20.

Dunstan Massey OSB
Westminster Abbey AD MMII

CURRICULM VITAE

My curriculum undoubtedly begins with a birthday in Vancouver, April 16th, 1924, and a little later with a Baptism, when I was named William Harold. At six I attended St. Patrick's private Grammar School and from 1930 to 1937 was taught by the Sisters of St. Joseph of Toronto, and studied piano with the Toronto Conservatory. I had barely set foot in high school when I decided (amazingly with parental permission) that I would prefer to study art rather than algebra. This was pursued at the Vancouver School of Art with Jack Shadbolt in 1938 and with Faulkner-Smith from the Slade School in London from 1939-41. During this interval, under the impetus of serious reading and reflection (Montalembert's *Monks of the West* and St. Bernard of Clairvaux's treatise *On the Love of God*), I decided despite all protestations of art and music teachers to 'throw my life away' in a monastic cloister!

Entering the Seminary of Christ the King in 1942 I completed high school (with algebra), matriculating in 1946; continued the Liberal Arts program – English Literature, History, Latin, Greek, Retoric and Oratory – and the subject I found entrancing, Greek, Medieval and Modern Philosophy. I received the Bachelor of Arts degree in 1952. This was followed by the study of Theology (Dogmatic, Moral and Mystical); with Old and New Testament Scripture, Church History, Canon Law, Liturgy and Homiletics, leading to a Bachelor of Theology degree in 1956. In the meantime I had entered the Novitiate at Westminster, then a Priory; pronounced my first vows in 1950, receiving the religious name of Dunstan. My solemn Profession followed in 1953 and I was ordained to the Priesthood in 1955, at which time I was appointed vice-Rector in the Seminary of Christ the King.

Going back to the art school years, my being mentored by Shadbolt, a Modernist, Lawren Harris, a Theosophist, and Faulkner-Smith, an Academician, gave me a broad perspective of possible styles. Arthur Lismer offered to teach me if I could get back to Toronto (which I could not) and Jock MacDonald gave me the dour advice, 'If you want to be an artist, learn to suffer!' However, it was Gerald Tyler who proved the prophet. He suggested, 'You should paint tempera and then fresco!' Study and reading fired my imaginative bent toward myth, symbolism and sacred iconography. Since then I have attempted bridging the gulf between ancient and contemporary forms.

In 1940 at age 16 I had my first one-man show in the Vancouver Art Gallery. There were Romantic incursions also in the B.C. Artists Annual with a water-colour allegory, *Spring*, and a Wagnerian ink drawing, *Brunnhilde's Immolation*. During my high school years I directed scenes from Macbeth and Faust. Under a brief fascination with the Beuronese school I painted The *Death of St. Joseph*, a 7'6" x 7' oil, large for me at the time, but The *Hound of Heaven*, an enormous tempera 32' x 25' foreshadowed, unfortunately only on paper, my muralistic yearnings. It was the backdrop for a choral recitation I directed in 1947 of Thompson's great poem. Undoubtedly influenced by the poet, I was writing lyric odes at the same time.

Just before the monastery and school moved to Mission in 1954 I was designing sixteen 4' x 6' reliefs of biblical animals, to be poured in concrete with the ceiling of our new common room. During the next 25 years art projects came on in spates: murals, oil on panel, *The Tree of Life* (11' x 36') and *The Miraculous Draft of Fish* (14' by 9'); then a 10' x 25' acrylic mural on plaster, *Curing the Blind Man*. Other works included a life-size ceramic *Crucifixion with two Angels*; a stained-glass window for the tower crypt and finally, fulfilling Gerry Tyler's injunction, three 5'6" x 2'8" egg-tempera panels of the *Life of St. Benedict*. After six years' preparation, as if to complete my good friend's mandate, I began a first fresco, the 10' x 15' *Temptation of St. Benedict*, in 1974. Concurrently I taught drama, directing classical works: Sophocles' *Electra*, Shakespeare's *Julius Caesar*, Coleridge's *The Rime of the Ancient Mariner*, Péguy's *Mystery of the Holy Innocents*, Osbert Sitwell's *Wrack at Tidesend*, 'Before the Law' from Kafka's *Trial*, and an experimental *Port Lliggat*, fusing Dali, poetry, slides and actors. I concluded this phase with Dante, an *Episodic Inferno* in 1975.

Rory Ralston curated a multimedia exhibition of mine at the University of British Columbia, called *Inner Dialogue*, in 1972. It dramatized the drawings for *The Temptation* fresco with sound, film projection and actors. We also collaborated in developing the film *Crown of Fire* which grew out of the exhibition and which was completed only in 1995-96 with Stephen Jones, when computers made possible the complex animation. *Crown of Fire* won the Golden Eagle at the Cine Awards in Washington D.C. in 1998.

With the building of the Abbey Church I was commissioned to make 22 life-size scenes from the lives of the saints in cast cement. Begun in 1980, they were completed in 1994. Meanwhile, through the years, I continued writing: lyric poems, *Vigils for a Watchman*, 1971, and *The Stone Ship*, a poetic drama in 1989. My illustrated epic poem *The Mystic Mountain* was completed in 1991. As this book goes to press I am beginning a large fresco, 31' by 20' for the monastic refectory. It is called the *Celestial Banquet*. Preparation began for it in 1978, and the work will be finished, God willing, in 2004.

ADMMII